Revitalizing Education

The Role of Academic Law Caveats in Student Growth

Aaron W. Wemple

Life Winks LLC

Contents

To all the students who have faced challenges in their legal education journey, this book is dedicated to you. Your resilience and determination to succeed despite the obstacles have inspired us to continue seeking solutions to improve the legal education system. We hope this book will empower and support you in your endeavors, and we stand with you in your quest for a more inclusive and equitable legal profession.

Introduction

Education is in flux, with critics concerned about its effectiveness in preparing students for future legal practice. Many people believe that the traditional approach to legal education does not develop the reasoning and critical thinking skills required for success. Many students find themselves unprepared for the real world after completing traditional legal education.

To address these concerns, parents, educators, and institutions have sought new and innovative approaches to legal education. Academic law caveats are one recent approach that has gained traction. These caveats, which are warnings or caveats about specific legal principles or doctrines, reimagines to encourage students to interact with and experience the law rather than memorize it.

Once upon a time, in a land far, far away, there was a young prince named Harold. Harold was the heir to the throne and was expected to become a great king one day. However, there was one problem: Harold didn't have a clue about how to rule a kingdom.

His parents, the King and Queen, were worried about their son's lack of knowledge about the legal system, so they decided to send him to the best law school in the land.

Harold was excited to start his legal education, but soon found out that the traditional approach to legal education was not for him. He spent hours memorizing laws and reading old court cases, but he couldn't see how it was relevant to his future role as a king.

One day, while Harold was daydreaming in class, he had a brilliant idea. He would create a new approach to legal education that would prepare students for the real world.

He approached his professors with his idea, but they laughed at him and told him it was impossible. Undeterred, Harold decided to take matters into his own hands.

He gathered a group of like-minded students and they began to create their own curriculum, focusing on developing reasoning and critical thinking skills. They also included real-world scenarios and case studies to make the education more relevant.

Word of Harold's new approach to legal education spread like wildfire, and soon, other law schools in the land were adopting his methods.

Harold graduated at the top of his class, and when he became king, he was able to rule with wisdom and fairness, thanks to his innovative approach to legal education.

This book, entitled "Revitalizing Education: The Role of Academic Law Caveats in Student Growth," aims to explore the use of academic law caveats to revitalize legal education. Through exams, looking closely at the key principles of engineering and physics law, as well as family law and family court law, this book will explore the challenges of traditional legal education and how academic law caveats can address these challenges. The book will provide examples of successful implementations of academic law caveats in legal education and consider future directions for legal education.

This book provides a comprehensive examination of the use of academic law caveats in legal. This book provides a comprehensive examination of the use of academic law caveats in legal education and the potential benefits they offer for student growth and development. We aim it at legal educators and institutions, as well as law students, legal practitioners, and anyone interested in designer education. The book will also explore the differences between engineering and physics law principles compared to family law and family court principles and how academic law caveats can help understand these areas of law.

Chapter One

Background on the Current State of Legal Education

"Real adaptiveness does not mean striving to always come out victorious or defeated, but rather embracing and learning from the experiences of both success and failure."

The field of legal education has undergone significant changes in recent years, as legal educators and institutions have questioned the effectiveness of traditional teaching methods. The way family law is taught is being scrutinized.

Legal education has emphasized the memorization and regurgitation of legal information, with little emphasis on the development of reasoning and critical thinking skills. They have criticized this approach for failing to prepare students for the practice of law, as well as for not developing the analytical skills needed for legal practice.

They have criticized traditional legal education for not being diverse enough and not addressing the structural inequalities that exist within the legal system.

In response to these criticisms, legal educators and institutions have looked for new and innovative ways to revitalize legal education. This has led to the emergence of alternative approaches, such as the use of experiential learning, problem-based learning, and the use of academic law caveats.

There is a focus on the importance of diversity in legal education. Many legal educators and institutions have addressed these issues through incorporating various initiatives, such as the use of diverse readings, incorporating the perspectives of marginalized groups, and increasing the representation of diverse faculty and students.

Amid this ongoing change and reevaluation, students can often find themselves confused and uncertain about the direction of legal education. Several students have shared stories about feeling overwhelmed by the sheer volume of information we expect them to learn and by the lack of emphasis on critical thinking and analysis. Some have reported feeling disconnected from the legal material they are learning, and unable to see the relevance of it to their future careers.

Jane, a second-year law student, said she has a hard time in her classes because she has to memorize many court cases but never gets to analyze or understand them. She also has trouble seeing how these cases will help her in her future job. She feels that her law school classes are not teaching her the skills she needs to be a talented lawyer.

Another student, Tom, a 3rd-year student, shared his experience of feeling disconnected and unengaged in his legal education. He felt that traditional teaching methods did not allow him to engage with the material and develop critical thinking skills. Tom found it difficult to apply the academic principles he was learning to real-world scenarios and saw a brief connection between his legal education and the practical aspects of legal practice.

Divorce courts have been facing a public crisis in recent years because of several factors, including increasing caseloads, limited resources, and changing societal norms. The ongoing litigation process can be a stressful and costly experience for families, and it can take a toll on the mental and emotional well-being of the parties involved, particularly children. The crisis in divorce courts has led to a growing need for new and innovative solutions that can help to streamline the process and make it more efficient and effective.

One of the major issues facing divorce courts is an increasing caseload. The legal system is strained because of more and more couples seeking divorce. This has led to delays in the court process, with some cases taking years to be resolved. The increasing caseload has led to a shortage of judges and court personnel, which further exacerbates the problem.

Another issue that students, schools, and divorce courts face is a lack of resources. Despite the growing caseload, many court clerks do not have the budget or staff to nurse the increased demand for their services. Delays and a lack of continuity in the court process can frustrate the parties. It can also lead to mistakes and oversights, which can have serious consequences for families.

Changes in society can cause problems in divorce courts. For example, people are more accepting of non-traditional families and valuing individual freedom more, which leads to more complex divorce cases about things like child custody, dividing property and supporting ex-spouses. The traditional court system may not handle these cases well. So, new and creative solutions are needed.

In response to this crisis, many courts are turning to alternative dispute resolution methods, such as mediation and collaborative law. These methods can be more efficient and effective than traditional court proceedings and can help to reduce the emotional and financial burden on families. For example, mediation allows couples to work out their differences in a confidential and non-adversarial setting, with the guidance of a neutral third party. Collaborative law is a process in which couples work together with their attorneys to reach a resolution that is mutually beneficial. Both methods have been effective in resolving disputes in a more amicable and cost-effective manner than traditional court proceedings.

Another policy being considered is the use of technology to help streamline the court process. Using online resources such as court forms, court calendars, and legal information can help to make the process more efficient and user-friendly.

One area of law that has traditionally been given less attention in legal education is family law. Although family law issues affect a significant portion of the population, we have traditionally seen the study of family law as less important than the study of more "substantive" areas of law such as contract, criminal or constitutional law.

The origins of this can be traced back to the early days of legal education, when law schools focused on training students for careers in corporate or government law. The traditional legal subjects that were important for these types of careers heavily influenced the curriculum of these early law schools, and family law was not among them. This is the reason they often considered the study of family law as a secondary or less important area of law.

The importance of family law in legal education has grown in recent years. As society has developed, so too has the nature of legal practice. The increasing complexity of family law issues, such as divorce, child custody, and domestic violence, has led to a growing demand for lawyers with expertise in this area of law.

This has led to a growing number of law schools to incorporate family law into their curriculum. These law schools recognize that family law is not only an important area of law but also an essential part of legal education. By studying family law, students can develop important skills such as negotiation, counseling, and problem-solving, skills that are not only important for a career in family law but also in any other area of legal practice.

In more recent years, there have been several innovative developments in family law that aim to make the legal process more efficient, effective, and user-friendly for families going through difficult and emotional times.

One such innovation is the use of "smart divorce contracts". These are contracts that are created using blockchain technology and smart contract functionality, which allows the terms of the divorce to be automatically executed based on predefined conditions. This can help streamline the divorce process and reduce the need for costly and time-consuming legal battles.

Another innovation in family law is the use of "constructive child safety files". These are digital files that are created by parents during the separation or divorce process, which contain important information about the children, such as their medical records, school information, and other important documents. They can share these files with the court and other relevant parties, such as attorneys and parenting coordinators, to help ensure the safety and well-being of the children throughout the legal process.

The use of AI-facilitated 360-degree mediations from multiple perspectives is a relatively new but promising innovation in family law. This technology analyzes data from multiple sources, such as court records, psychological evaluations, social worker recommendations, and others, to create a comprehensive picture of a family's situation. This allows the mediator to have a much more nuanced understanding of the family dynamics and issues at hand, which can help to facilitate more effective mediation and a better outcome for the children involved. It works well in cases where parents face chronic adversity and the legal process is difficult.

There are many innovative developments taking place in family law. These technologies are helping to make the legal process more efficient, effective, and user-friendly, and they are helping to ensure that the needs and well-being of the children are considered throughout the legal process.

Southern Illinois University-Edwardsville (SIUE) and other universities have integrated degrees that blend childhood psychology with STEM fields to support the development of new technologies and innovations in family law. These programs aim to provide students with a unique set of skills that are well-suited to addressing the complex issues that arise in family law, particularly those related to child safety and well-being.

One such innovation that universities like SIUE are working on is the development of "constructive child safety file" networks. These networks provide a secure and easy-to-use platform for sharing important information about children between parents, attorneys, and other relevant parties. The network makes use of Peer-to-peer technology, where the nodes on the network are connected directly to each other, rather than through a central server, making it a decentralized network.

Integrating childhood psychology into STEM fields is crucial for these networks, as it allows for the development of features that are specifically tailored to the needs of children. For example, by considering the developmental stage of a child and their specific needs, the network can ensure that the information shared is age appropriate and presented in a way that is easy for children to understand. By utilizing the latest technology such as blockchain, machine learning, artificial intelligence and others, the networks can ensure that the information shared is secure and tamper-proof, and that allowed parties in real-time can access it.

This type of program aims to provide students with a comprehensive understanding of both the technical and social aspects of these systems, preparing them for a career in which they can use these skills to help improve the legal process for families and children. Through integrating childhood psychology with STEM fields, students learn how to create tools that are child-centered and that consider the unique needs and perspectives of children, which is essential for the development of effective and user-friendly systems that prioritize the well-being of children.

In conclusion, family law and the current state of legal education is one of ongoing change and reevaluation, as legal educators and institutions seek new and innovative ways to improve the effectiveness of legal education and to address the challenges facing legal education. These students' stories underline the need for alternative approaches that focus on developing critical thinking skills and more practical and relevant education. This book aims to provide a comprehensive examination of the use of academic law caveats to revitalize legal education and address these challenges, and prepare students to succeed in their legal careers.

The previous chapter provided a background on the current state of legal education and the challenges it faces, particularly in family law. As we have seen, there is a growing need for new and innovative solutions that can help to address these challenges and improve the effectiveness of legal education. In this book, we aim to explore the use of academic law caveats to revitalize legal education, and in particular, the area of family law.

This book examines the role of academic law caveats in student growth and to provide an in-depth analysis of the use of these caveats to revitalize legal education. We will explore the various academic law caveats that are currently being used in legal education and how they can be effectively implemented. The book will also provide case studies and examples of how academic law caveats have been used in real-world settings to improve the effectiveness of legal education.

The scope of the book will focus on the use of academic law caveats in the area of family law, as it is an area that has traditionally been given less attention in legal education. We will examine the specific challenges that arise in family law and how academic law caveats can address these challenges. We will also discuss the importance of diversity and inclusion in legal education, and how academic law caveats can be used to promote these values.

In the following chapters, we will explore the various academic law caveats that are currently being used in legal education, including experiential learning, problem-based learning, and the use of technology. We will also examine how they can effectively implement how academic law caveats in legal education, including the importance of collaboration and interdisciplinary approaches. We will discuss how academic law caveats can promote diversity and inclusion in legal education.

In summary, this book aims to provide a comprehensive examination of the use of academic law caveats to revitalize legal education, and in particular, the area of family law. We will explore the various types of academic law caveats that are currently being used in legal education, the ways in which they can be effectively implemented, and the benefits that they can provide for students and legal education as a whole. Through the use of case studies and examples, we will demonstrate the real-world impact of academic law caveats on legal education and the ways in which they can be used to promote diversity and inclusion.

Chapter Two

Purpose and Scope of the Book

"Revitalization is not just about restoring the old, but about creating something new and even better."

In the previous chapter, we provided an overview of the current state of legal education and its challenges, particularly in family law. We also outlined the purpose and scope of this book, which is to examine the role of academic law caveats in student growth and to provide an in-depth analysis of these caveats' use to revitalize legal education, particularly in the area of family law.

Academic law caveats are innovative teaching methods designed to improve legal education's effectiveness by providing students with a more hands-on and practical learning experience. These methods include experiential learning, problem-based learning, and the use of technology. Academic law caveats are particularly useful in family law, as they can help address the specific challenges that arise in this area of law.

Three examples of student's experiences:

Example 1: John is a 2nd-year law student struggling with the traditional teaching methods in his legal education. He needs help understanding and applying the legal principles he is learning to real-world scenarios. However, after participating in an experiential learning program, John found a better understanding of using the legal principles known. The program provided him with real-world experience in a legal setting, which allowed him to see the relevance of the legal principles he was learning.

Example 2: Sarah is a 3rd-year law student interested in pursuing a career in family law. She has found traditional legal education to be disconnected from the practical aspects of legal practice. However, after participating in a problem-based learning program, Sarah found that she could better understand the complexities of family law. The program provided her with a problem-based learning experience that allowed her to apply the legal principles she was learning to real-world situations and scenarios. She also appreciated the emphasis placed on understanding the perspective of the families and children involved in family law cases which helped her develop essential skills such as negotiation, counseling, and problem-solving.

Example 3: David is a 4th-year law student who found traditional legal education dry and tedious. He was excited to hear about the law school's pilot program that uses technology to enhance the legal education experience. He found that using online resources, such as legal simulations, virtual reality, and e-learning platforms, made learning more interactive and engaging. Additionally, AI facilitated 360-degree mediation from multiple perspectives and gave him a more nuanced understanding of the family dynamics and issues at play.

These examples demonstrate how academic law caveats, such as experiential learning, problem-based learning, and technology use, can improve the effectiveness of legal education, particularly in the area of family law. These methods provide students with a more hands-on and practical learning experience, allowing them to understand and apply the legal principles they are learning. Additionally, the use of academic law caveats promotes the use of diverse perspectives and encourages the development of essential skills such as negotiation, counseling, and problem-solving.

Once upon a time, a law student named Jane struggled to keep up with her studies. She found the traditional teaching methods in her legal education to be dry and dull. She needed help understanding and applying the legal principles she was learning to real-world scenarios.

One day, as she was flipping through her textbooks, she stumbled upon a mysterious chapter in her family law textbook entitled "Revitalizing Education: The Role of Academic Law Caveats in Student Growth." Intrigued, she decided to give it a read.

As she delved deeper into the chapter, she was surprised to find that it was filled with humorous anecdotes about confused law students and innovative solutions to the challenges faced by legal education, particularly in the area of family law. She couldn't help but laugh as she read about the use of "smart divorce contracts" and "constructive child safety files" to streamline the divorce process, and the use of AI facilitated 360-degree mediations from multiple perspectives to provide a more nuanced understanding of family dynamics.

Feeling inspired, Jane sought out her professors and asked if they could incorporate some of these innovative teaching methods into her legal education. Her professors were initially skeptical, but after seeing these methods' positive impact on Jane's understanding and engagement, they decided to try them.

Soon, other students at the law school began to notice the changes and followed Jane's lead, and before long, the entire law school had embraced the use of academic law caveats in their legal education. The students found the classes more attractive and engaging and, most importantly, helped them understand the legal principles better and apply them to real-world scenarios.

The result was a law school filled with well-prepared, motivated, and happy law students ready to take on the challenges of the legal profession with confidence. And as for Jane, she found herself at the top of her class, and she knew that her success was all thanks to that mysterious new book that had sparked her curiosity and changed her life forever.

Please remember that while I tried to make the story humorous, it still needs to be placed that the book's primary focus is serious and is meant to improve legal education. These techniques and tools can help students better understand and apply legal principles while providing a more engaging and interactive learning experience.

In the next chapter, we will delve deeper into the specific types of academic law caveats currently being used in legal education, including experiential learning, problem-based learning, and the use of technology. We will examine how these methods can be effectively implemented in legal education and provide examples of how they have been used in real-world settings to improve the effectiveness of legal education. Additionally, we will explore the potential of technology and AI in providing new and innovative ways of teaching and learning in legal education.

Chapter Three

The Fundamentals of Legal Education

To understand the role of academic law caveats in student growth, it is important first to understand the fundamentals of legal education. Legal education plays a crucial role in preparing students for a career in the legal profession and is designed to provide students with the knowledge, skills, and values needed to be practical and ethical legal professionals.

Legal education typically begins with a foundational curriculum that covers the basics of the legal system, including the Constitution, criminal law, and contracts. This foundation curriculum is designed to give students a general understanding of the legal system and the basic principles of the law.

As students progress through their legal education, they typically take more specialized courses that focus on specific areas of law, such as family law, intellectual property law, and tax law. These specialized courses are designed to give students a deeper understanding of the legal principles and practices that apply to these areas of law.

In addition to the knowledge and skills students gain from their legal education, legal education also emphasizes the development of values and professional responsibilities. Legal education programs typically include courses on legal ethics, professional responsibility, and the lawyer's role in society. These courses are designed to teach students about the ethical and professional standards that apply to the legal profession and the importance of serving the public interest.

However, despite its importance, legal education has been criticized in recent years for needing to be updated, connected to the practical aspects of legal practice, and providing students with the skills they need to be influential legal professionals. This is where academic law caveats come in; they can address these issues by providing students with a more hands-on and practical learning experience.

Experiential learning is an academic law caveat that can provide students with real-world experience in a legal setting. Experiential learning provides students with the opportunity to develop practical skills such as problem-solving, negotiation, and communication, which are essential for success in the legal profession. This type of learning includes simulations, clinics, externships, and mock trials that allow students to apply the legal principles they are learning to real-world situations.

The fundamentals of any college major will vary depending on the specific field of study. However, generally speaking, the fundamentals of any college major can be broken down into several key areas:

1. Core Curriculum: This typically includes the foundational courses that are required for the major. These courses provide students with a basic understanding of the principles and concepts central to the field of study.

2. Specialized courses: As students progress through their major, they typically take more specialized courses that focus on specific topics within the field. These courses build upon the foundation established in the core curriculum and provide students with a deeper understanding of the field.

3. Research and Project work: Many college majors also require students

to complete research projects or internships as part of their studies. This allows students to apply the knowledge and skills acquired in the classroom to real-world situations and gain practical experience in the field.

4. Applied and experiential learning: some college majors may require students to participate in hands-on, real-world experience, such as clinics, lab work, internships, or co-ops, which will help students gain practical and theoretical knowledge and expose them to different situations.

5. Additional support courses: Some majors may require additional courses such as language courses, mathematics, statistics, or computer courses to support the primary curriculum.

6. Graduation Requirement: Each college major has its graduation requirements. This includes completing a certain number of credit hours, maintaining a minimum GPA, passing specific classes, and completing a capstone project or thesis.

It's worth noting that the specifics of what constitutes the fundamentals of a college major will vary depending on the field of study. However, this broad overview provides a general idea of what one can expect when pursuing any college major.

Problem-based learning is another academic law caveat that can be effective in legal education. This method involves presenting students with legal problems or scenarios and asking them to work together to find solutions. This approach emphasizes the importance of understanding the perspectives of all parties involved and using critical thinking and problem-solving skills. It also allows students to apply the legal principles they are learning to real-world situations and to gain a deeper understanding of the complexities of the law.

Family courthouses manage the legal proceedings related to family law matters, such as divorce, child custody, and adoption. They are not primarily focused on providing educational resources or guidance to students. Family courthouses may not warn students about the potential differences between scientific laws and family law principles because they are typically focused on providing legal services and handling legal cases rather than providing educational resources or guidance to students.

Additionally, the training and education of law students are typically the responsibility of law schools rather than the courthouses. Law schools are better equipped to provide students with the knowledge and skills necessary to understand the nuances of different areas of law, including the potential differences between scientific laws and family law principles.

Furthermore, many family court cases are emotionally charged and complex. The focus of these cases is often to resolve legal issues related to families and children and to do so in the child's best interest. This is why the court may need more guidance or resources for students on reconciling scientific laws with the complexities of family law and cases.

Family law cases tend to differ from scientific ones, requiring an understanding of family dynamics, psychology, and other social sciences, which may require more work to combine and reconcile with scientific laws. Some students may experience frustration and confusion as they attempt to reconcile the two bodies of knowledge and understanding of the law and feel torn when applying scientific rules to the real-world complexities and nuances of family law cases.

While family courthouses are focused on providing legal services and handling legal cases, they may need more resources or capability to provide students with the guidance and resources they need to reconcile the differences between scientific laws and family law principles. Law schools must provide students with the necessary educational resources and advice and help them navigate the complexities of different areas of law.

Technology is another academic law caveat that can be used to enhance the effectiveness of legal education. Online resources such as legal simulations, virtual reality, and e-learning platforms can make learning more interactive and engaging. Additionally, AI-facilitated mediation and legal research can provide students with new and innovative ways of understanding the law and legal practice.

In conclusion, academic law caveats provide students with a more hands-on, practical, and engaging learning experience. They are particularly effective in family law, where they can help address specific challenges such as working with diverse perspectives, promoting child-centered solutions, and providing a more nuanced understanding of family dynamics. These methods can be integrated with a legal education to supplement traditional teaching methodologies, providing law students with a comprehensive knowledge of the law and the legal profession.

Chapter Four

Overview of the Legal Education System

"Be sure to put your feet in the right place, and then stand firm" - Abraham Lincoln.

The legal education system plays a vital role in developing future legal professionals. It is designed to provide students with the knowledge and skills necessary to understand and apply the law. However, the legal education system has come under scrutiny in recent years, with concerns about its ability to prepare students for the realities of legal practice. This chapter will provide an overview of the legal education system, including its history, structure, and current issues.

History of legal education

The history of legal education dates back to the Middle Ages when law students would receive apprenticeships under a practicing lawyer. The apprenticeship system was the primary method of legal education until the 19th century when law schools emerged as separate institutions from universities. The first law school in the United States was established in 1779.

In the 20th century, legal education underwent significant changes. The American Bar Association (ABA) and the Association of American Law Schools (AALS) established accreditation standards for law schools, which set guidelines for the curriculum, faculty qualifications, and library resources. In addition, the ABA and AALS established standards for the length of legal education, which required a minimum of three years of full-time study for the JD degree.

Structure of legal education

The structure of legal education in the United States is based on the JD degree, a professional doctorate in law. The JD degree is required for those who wish to practice law in the United States. It is divided into two parts: the first two years, referred to as the "first-year curriculum," focus on the study of foundational legal concepts, while the final year, referred to as the "upper-level curriculum," focuses on specialized areas of law.

The legal education system also includes graduate programs such as the LLM (Master of Laws) and the SJD (Doctor of Juridical Science), typically for students who have already completed the JD degree and want to specialize in a specific area of law or pursue an academic career.

Current issues in legal education

Despite its long history and established structure, the legal education system is facing several challenges in recent years, including:

- Cost: The cost of legal education has risen significantly in recent years, making it difficult for many students to afford it. This has led to concerns about the student debt crisis and its impact on the legal profession.

- Lack of practical training: Some critics argue that the legal education system needs to provide more practical training to prepare students for the realities of legal practice. They say that law schools should offer more opportunities for students to gain valuable experience through internships and clinics.

- Lack of diversity: The legal profession is still dominated by white men, and law schools have been criticized for not doing enough to promote diversity and inclusion.

- A decrease in enrollment in law schools has also been a concern in recent years, with many schools experiencing a decline in the number of students enrolling. This has led to financial challenges for law schools and raised questions about legal education's future.

- Relevance to the job market: The legal job market is highly competitive and has changed significantly in recent years. As a result, law graduates may find it difficult to secure employment after graduation and may struggle to find jobs that match their skills and interests. This has led to concerns about the relevance of legal education to the job market.

- Lack of specialization: Some law schools may not offer enough specialized courses that can make the students ready for specific fields. Thus the students may lack the knowledge and skills required for particular areas of practice such as intellectual property, criminal law, family law, etc.

- Limited exposure to technology and science-based principles: With the evolution of technology and science-based principles, law students have lacked exposure in these fields. This could limit their ability to work on cases that involve advanced technology and scientific laws.

An example of a closed law school is the Whittier Law School in Costa Mesa, California. The school was founded in 1966 and was fully accredited by the American Bar Association (ABA). However, due to financial difficulties and a decline in enrollment, the Whittier College Board of Trustees decided to stop conducting recruitment and enrollment activities in April 2017. In July 2020, Whittier Law School will shut down completely.

The school's declining enrollment was due in part to a national trend of decreasing enrollment in law schools. In addition, the school had struggled financially for several years and could not secure the funding necessary to continue operations. Despite efforts to find a merger partner or buyer, the school ultimately could not secure the resources needed to continue operating.

The closure of Whittier Law School was difficult for students, faculty, and staff. The students were assisted in transferring to other law schools, and the faculty and staff were provided with support as they looked for new opportunities. The closure of this school serves as a reminder of the challenges facing the legal education system and the importance of addressing these challenges to ensure the success of future law students and legal professionals.

A university's closure can significantly impact the students, faculty, staff, and the surrounding community. Universities close for various reasons, such as financial difficulties, lack of enrollment, and changing societal needs. Economic challenges can include a lack of funding from government sources, decreased philanthropic donations, or a lack of endowments. A decrease in enrollment can be caused by a variety of factors, such as a decrease in the population of high school graduates in the area, increased competition from other colleges and universities, or a change in societal needs that results in a decrease in interest in a particular field of study. Additionally, universities may close if they cannot adapt to changes in technology, societal needs, or shifting economic conditions.

University boards and donors are responsible for making strategic decisions that guide the institution's direction and ensure its long-term sustainability. However, they need to notice the changing times and shifting societal needs, which can lead to the decline of the university. For example, a university may focus intensely on a specific field of study, but as society's needs change, that field may no longer be in high demand. With the proper adaptation, the university may be able to attract students and secure funding. Additionally, as technology and online learning platforms advance, universities may fail to adapt and adopt these innovations, making them less attractive to students who prefer more flexible and convenient learning options. This inability to adapt to changing times can lead to a decline in enrollment, resulting in financial difficulties and, ultimately, the university's closure.

Once upon a time, there was a college law professor named Professor Smith. He had taught for many years and was highly respected in the legal community. However, when the Covid-19 pandemic hit, everything changed. Classes were moved online, and Professor Smith needed help to adapt. He had never used the digital blackboard before, and the technology was utterly foreign to him.

The students in Professor Smith's class were eager to learn, but they quickly realized the course would be challenging. Professor Smith would spend most of the class time figuring out how to use the digital blackboard, leaving little time for actual instruction. He could not accept homework assignments digitally, and the students were left to figure out how to submit their work independently.

The students were frustrated, and their grades began to suffer. Many of them flunked the class. Professor Smith was devastated. He had never had a class fail before, and he couldn't understand why this was happening. He reached out to the students for feedback, but it was too late. The damage had been done and would live on in the school record books, missing from future professional records for all time.

The semester ended, and the students moved on to try and rebound in other classes. Professor Smith was left to reflect on what had gone wrong. He realized that he needed to take the time to learn how to use the digital blackboard correctly and that his lack of technology skills had significantly impacted his students. He committed himself to learn more about technology and better adapt to the changing times.

The consequences of all the students in Professor Smith's class flunking out due to his lack of knowledge on the digital blackboard were far-reaching and had a significant impact on their futures.

Firstly, the academic navigation of the students was stopped or greatly influenced. Many could not move on to the next level of their education because they had failed a required course. This put them behind schedule and forced them to retake the class, which added additional time and expenses to their education.

Some students were so discouraged that they decided to drop out of law school altogether, causing them to lose out on their dream of becoming a lawyer.

Secondly, the student's professional careers were also affected. Many of them could not secure internships or job opportunities as they had failed an essential class in their field. This disadvantaged them when competing for jobs with peers who had yet to encounter the same difficulties.

Finally, the student's personal and emotional well-being were impacted. The stress and disappointment of failing a class, especially during a challenging time like the Covid-19 pandemic, took a toll on their mental and emotional health. Many experienced anxiety, depression, and hopelessness, which affected their relationships and overall well-being.

The failure of all students in Professor Smith's class due to his lack of knowledge of digital tools had a ripple effect that changed their academic and professional lives forever. This highlights the importance of adapting to the changing times and constantly updating skills, especially in the digital era, to ensure success for educators and students.

The differences in legal school structures is the comparison between traditional and online law schools. Conventional family law schools, also known as brick-and-mortar law schools, offer classes on a physical campus, and students must attend classes in person. These schools typically follow a traditional semester schedule, with classes held during the fall and spring semesters and a break during the summer. In addition, conventional law schools often have a set curriculum that students must complete to graduate.

On the other hand, online law schools offer classes primarily or entirely online and do not have a physical campus. Students can access classes and course materials remotely and may have more flexibility regarding when and where they complete their coursework. Online law schools also often have more flexible schedules and may offer classes year-round. Some online law schools may also have a self-paced curriculum or allow students to design their curriculum, giving more freedom and flexibility in terms of what courses the student chooses to take.

Another example of the difference is the "law and" schools, which are law schools that are integrative with other fields of study such as business, medicine, or science. These law schools generally have a curriculum that includes courses on legal topics and approaches from different fields of study. This structure will prepare students to practice law in specialized areas such as health, intellectual property, or international business law.

Once upon a time, a law student named Bob dreamed of becoming a top lawyer in engineering and physics law. Bob was a diligent student with a strong science background but needed more emphasis on engineering and physics in his law school curriculum.

One day, Bob had had enough and decided to take matters into his own hands. He decided to sneak into the physics lab at night and conduct experiments on his own. But things didn't go as planned, and Bob accidentally created a black hole in the lab. The Dean of the law school stumbled upon the black hole and was sucked in, never to be seen again.

Bob was immediately expelled from the law school for his reckless behavior but decided not to let this setback discourage him. He realized that the only way to excel in engineering and physics law indeed was to combine his knowledge of science with his understanding of the law.

He could finally apply his scientific knowledge to legal problems and understand the intricacies of cases that dealt with advanced technology and scientific principles. So, he enrolled in an interdisciplinary program that offered engineering, physics, child psychology, and law courses. The program was unique and challenging, but Bob was determined to succeed.

Bob graduated with distinction and became a highly sought-after lawyer in engineering and physics law. He also wrote a book on the subject, titled "Bob's Guide to Engineering and Physics Law," which became a best-seller and was even adopted as a textbook in some law schools.

Bob's story serves as a reminder that the critical principles of engineering and physics law are essential for legal professionals to understand and effectively handle complex cases in this field fully. And it also reminds us that sometimes, you have to think out of the box and take some risks, even if it means being expelled from law school and almost creating a black hole!

With that said, Bob's experience serves as a prelude to chapter 4, where the key principles of engineering and physics law will be discussed in detail. Through this chapter, the reader will understand how these principles can be integrated into legal education and practice to improve client outcomes and provide more effective legal education.

In conclusion, the legal education system is facing various challenges, including rising costs, a lack of practical training, diversity, a decrease in enrollment, relevance to the job market, a lack of specialization, and limited exposure to technology and science-based principles. These challenges have led to concerns about the future of legal education and the ability of law schools to prepare students for the realities of legal practice. However, with the proper attention and resources, it is possible to address these challenges and ensure that the legal education system continues to provide students with the knowledge and skills necessary to succeed as legal professionals.

Chapter Five

Key Principles of Engineering and Physics Law

"Any idiot can build a bridge that stands, but it takes an engineer to build a bridge that barely stands." - Unknown.

Once upon a time, there was a girl named Olivia. She was a curious and ambitious young woman who had always been fascinated by the world around her. Growing up, she loved to explore the city, climbing to the top of buildings and bridges to get a better view of the world below.

As she got older, Olivia became more and more interested in understanding how the structures she loved to explore were built. She studied engineering in college, learning about the fundamental principles of physics and its use in designing and constructing buildings and other structures.

One day, Olivia stumbled upon a book about the engineering of skyscrapers, bridges, and smartphones. She was immediately drawn to the subject matter and began reading the book with great interest.

As she read, Olivia learned about the various technologies and innovations that have enabled the construction of taller and more advanced structures. She was particularly fascinated by how engineers use statics and dynamics principles to ensure these structures' safety and stability under various loads and conditions.

Olivia was also fascinated by the material properties and strength and how engineers use these principles to ensure the safety and stability of these structures under various loads and conditions.

Olivia's interest in the book was not only academic but also personal. She has always been interested in how the world around her works and how it can be improved, and she knew that this knowledge would be valuable in her future career as an engineer.

In the end, Olivia finished the book with a deeper understanding of the scientific and technical aspects of engineering and physics and how they are applied to create the structures that we rely on in our daily lives. She knew this knowledge would be invaluable in her future career, and she couldn't wait to put it into practice.

As she closed the book, Olivia couldn't help but look out the window, her gaze drawn to the city's towering skyscrapers. She knew that there was still so much more to learn, and she couldn't wait to dive in and explore the world of engineering and physics even further.

This chapter will delve into the underlying principles that form the foundation of engineering and physics. We will explore how these fundamental laws are applied in the design and construction of some of the most iconic structures of our time, such as skyscrapers, bridges, and smartphones. We will cover topics such as statics and dynamics, material properties and strength, and how engineers use these principles to ensure the safety and stability of these structures under various loads and conditions. Additionally, we will discuss the different technologies and innovations that have enabled the construction of taller and more advanced facilities and how they have shaped the built environment around us. Overall, this chapter aims to provide a deeper understanding of engineering and physics scientific and technical aspects and how they are applied to create the structures that we rely on in our daily lives.

Newton's First Law, also known as the Law of Inertia, explains how an object's movement is affected by the balance of forces acting upon it. In science, the term "law" refers to a generalization that describes a specific aspect of the natural world. This is different from legal laws found in family law schools or industries. Scientific laws are supported by evidence and can be described as a theory, a well-supported explanation of a specific feature of the natural world. A theory can include facts, laws, inferences, and testable hypotheses. Theories are subject to testing and can be amended or abandoned if found to be flawed. Newton's first law states that an object at rest will remain at rest, and an object in motion will continue at a constant speed unless acted upon by an unbalanced external force.

The work of Galileo in the 16th century significantly advanced the field of science, particularly in the area of mechanics. Galileo was a scientist who lived a long time ago. He helped figure out how things move and how they work. He was like a detective trying to solve a mystery. Later, another scientist named Newton also studied how things move. He built on what Galileo discovered and helped us understand how things work in the world around us.

Similarly, Newton's contributions continued to unearth the boundaries of scientific understanding in this field, particularly in his focus on experimental science and the mechanics of moving objects.

Newton's three laws of motion, also known as the laws of classical mechanics, are a set of fundamental principles describing the relationship between a body's motion and its forces. These laws were first formulated by Sir Isaac Newton in the late 17th century and are considered some of the most important laws in physics.

Newton's three laws of motion are like a set of rules that tell us how things move. They help us understand why things move the way they do when forces act on them. Just like how we have rules for playing different games, these laws help us understand how things move in the world around us. They are used in many different fields, like building robots or exploring space. A long time ago, a man named Galileo helped discover these rules. Later, another man named Newton built on Galileo's work and helped us understand even more about how things move or stay in place.

The first law, known as the Law of Inertia, states that an object at rest will remain at rest, and an object in motion will continue at a constant speed in a straight line unless acted upon by an unbalanced external force. This principle is often referred to as the "inertial reference frame" and is the foundation for studying dynamics.

A fun example of Newton's First Law of Motion, also known as the Law of Inertia, is a roller coaster ride. As the roller coaster cars are pulled up the first hill, they are at rest. According to the Law of Inertia, an object at rest will remain at rest unless acted upon by an unbalanced force. Once the cars reach the top of the hill, gravity takes over and acts as the unbalanced force, causing the cars to begin moving. As the cars move through the twists and turns of the roller coaster track, they continue in motion until they reach the end of the ride and come to a stop, once again at rest.

The second law, known as the Law of Mass and Acceleration, states that the acceleration of an object is directly proportional to the net force acting upon it and inversely proportional to its mass. This principle is often represented by the equation $F = ma$, where F is the force, m is the mass, and a is the acceleration.

A fun example of Newton's Second Law, also known as the Law of Mass and Acceleration, is a game of bowling. When the bowler releases the bowling ball, the ball is at rest. According to the Law of Mass and Acceleration, the acceleration of an object is directly proportional to the net force acting on the object and inversely proportional to its mass.

As the bowler applies force to the ball by pushing it down the lane, the ball begins to accelerate, gaining speed as it goes. The heavier the ball, the more force is needed to accelerate it to the same speed as a lighter ball.

When the ball reaches the end of the lane, it collides with the pins, exerting a force on them and causing them to move, which is acceleration. The bigger the force, the more the pins will move and more likely to knock down all of them.

So, the second law of motion is demonstrated in this example as the force exerted by the bowler on the ball, the ball's mass, and the ball's acceleration all contribute to the game's outcome (with or without record books.

The third law, known as the Third Law of Motion, states that for every action, there is an equal and opposite reaction. This principle is often referred to as the "action-reaction principle" and is the foundation for the study of rocket propulsion and the behavior of gasses.

A fun example of Newton's Third Law of Motion, also known as the Law of Action and Reaction, is a rocket launch. According to the Law of Action and Reaction, there is an equal and opposite reaction for every action.

When a rocket is launching, the engines at the bottom of the rocket emit hot gasses out of the back, creating thrust that propels the projectile upwards. The action is the force of the hot gasses being expelled from the rocket, pushing the rocket in the opposite direction (upwards). The reaction to this action is the rocket moving upwards.

As the rocket continues to burn fuel, the thrust continues to push the rocket higher and faster into the atmosphere. The greater the thrust, the greater the force driving the rocket upwards, and the greater the reaction of the rocket moving upwards.

The action of the hot gasses being expelled from the rocket and the reaction of the rocket moving upwards demonstrate the Third Law of Motion.

In summary, Newton's three laws of motion are an essential part of the study of physics, and these laws are considered facts in the scientific community. They provide a framework for understanding how objects move and how forces affect their motion, and they continue to be used in many fields, including engineering, robotics, and space exploration.

Skyscraper design

Around 350 years ago, Sir Isaac Newton's "Laws" characterized the physical universe on a massive scale. He referred to them as principles, but we now refer to them as laws. Newton's three laws must be understood before building things because they all directly affect structures.

Designing a skyscraper involves a complex array of engineering and physics principles. From the foundation to the top of the building, engineers and architects must consider factors such as load-bearing capacity, structural integrity, and wind resistance. One fundamental principle of engineering and physics law that applies to skyscraper design is the principle of safety. Engineers and architects must ensure that their blueprints meet safety standards and codes to prevent harm to the building's occupants and the public.

For example, in the design of a skyscraper, engineers must consider the effects of seismic activity, wind loads, and fire hazards. They must also take into account the ongoing needs and safety of the building's inhabitants in case of emergency, such as providing emergency exits, fire suppression systems, and other safety measures.

When an engineer named Nancy designs her skyscrapers, she has to consider many factors to ensure the structure's safety and stability. This includes analyzing the load-bearing capacity of the building's materials, determining the most efficient distribution of weight, and calculating wind and seismic loads to ensure the structure can withstand natural forces. One of the most critical tasks she must undertake is to apply the laws of physics to the design, using computer-aided drafting (CAD) systems to create detailed plans and simulations. Using CAD software, she will create detailed blueprints and models of the building, taking into account factors such as structural integrity, energy efficiency, and fire safety. They will also use the software to simulate different scenarios and stress test the building's design, making any necessary adjustments to ensure it meets all safety and building codes. Nancy works closely with architects, builders, and engineers throughout the design process to ensure the final design meets customer expectations. Plus, it is safe for all, structurally sound, and aesthetically pleasing.

Bridge design

Bridge design also involves a complex array of engineering and physics principles. Engineers must consider factors such as load-bearing capacity, structural integrity, and resistance to environmental conditions. Key principles of engineering and physics law that apply to bridge design include the regulation of safety and the principles of working with nature and environmental protection.

For example, engineers must consider the effects of environmental conditions such as flooding, ice and snow, and wind loads on the bridge's structure. They must also ensure that the bridge design meets safety standards, including load-bearing capacity and structural integrity, to prevent harm to the public and the bridge's users.

Once upon a time, an engineer named John was tasked with designing a bridge over a vast and fast-moving river. He was an experienced designer and had built many bridges in the past, so he felt confident that he could design one that would be both beautiful and safe.

John began working on the design, using computer-aided drafting (CAD) systems to create detailed plans and simulations. He calculated the load-bearing capacity of the materials and determined the most efficient distribution of weight. He also considered the effects of wind and water on the bridge. However, there was one thing John forgot to take into account: the soil beneath the riverbed.

As the bridge construction began, everything was going well. The workers were making steady progress, and the bridge was taking shape. But as the days passed, the river's water level started to rise. John was worried, but he thought that the bridge would hold. He was wrong.

One night, the bridge washed away as the river reached its highest level. The soil beneath the riverbed was weak and unable to support the bridge's weight. The workers were devastated, and John was filled with remorse. He knew that the disaster could have been avoided if he had only remembered to test the soil before building the bridge.

John learned a valuable lesson that day. He realized that even the most experienced engineers can make monumental mistakes and that it's always essential to test and verify all factors, no matter how small, before beginning a construction project.

Only after bridges wash away do we realize we had made a mistake by not checking the strength of the ground under the river before building the bridge. John learned that ensuring the foundation is strong enough to hold up the bridge is very important. So from then on, before creating any bridges, he always checked the strength of the ground first, like a doctor checking if a bone was healthy before surgery. He always wanted to avoid making the same mistake again and ensure all structures he designs are safe and robust.

Bridges need to be able to resist a variety of forces (Boon et al., 2021). Pushing and pulling, or compression and tension, are the two most frequently used models of bridges. Shear and torsion (twisting) make up the other two. Discover the significance of these forces to improve your model bridge construction.

In addition, engineers must also consider the environmental impact of bridge maintenance. This includes measures like future painting to prevent rust and metal guards from preserving wildlife and natural habitats around the bridge.

Smartphone and cellular transmission design

The laws of electricity play a crucial role in the design and functionality of smartphones and cellular transmission.

Ohm's law states that the current flowing through a conductor is directly proportional to its voltage and inversely proportional to its resistance. This law is used in designing the electrical circuits within smartphones to ensure that the appropriate amount of current flows through the circuit to power the various components of the phone, such as the screen, processor, and battery.

Okay, kiddo, so you know how your phone works, right? It has a battery that gives it power and different parts like the screen and the phone's brain that need that power to work. Ohm's law is like a rule that helps make sure the right amount of power gets to all those parts. It says that if we give the phone more power, it will flow through it. But if the phone has more "blockers" to the electricity, like a bigger "resistor," less electricity will flow. This rule helps the people who make phones make sure everything works well.

Kirchhoff's laws, which include Kirchhoff's current law (KCL) and Kirchhoff's voltage law (KVL), are used to analyze and predict the behavior of electrical circuits. KCL states that the total current entering a node in a circuit must equal the total current leaving the node, while KVL states that the total voltage around any closed loop in a circuit must be zero. These laws are used to design and optimize the electrical circuits within smartphones to ensure that they are efficient and have minimal losses.

Faraday's law of electromagnetic induction states that a changing magnetic field induces an electromotive force (EMF) in a conductor. This law is used in designing smartphones and cellular transmission tower antennas to ensure they can effectively transmit and receive signals.

Okay, kiddo, how can you use your phone to talk to your friends and family, even if they're far away? Like magic! Well, that's not magic; it's science! And Faraday's law is a big part of how it works. It's like when you're playing with your toy cars, and you have a long ramp, and you roll a car down it; the car goes faster and faster right? Faraday's law is like that but with magnets and electricity. When the magnets in your phone's antenna move around or change, it makes electricity move too. And that's how your phone talks to other phones and the big towers you see everywhere, like rolling toy cars down a ramp, only with magnets and electricity.

A fun example of how these laws are used in smartphones is the camera's design. In a camera, the image sensor converts light into electrical signals. Ohm's law ensures that the appropriate amount of current flows through the circuit to power the image sensor. Kirchhoff's laws are used to analyze the circuit and optimize the design for minimal losses. Faraday's law is used in the antenna design to ensure that the image can be transmitted to the user's device.

In summary, the laws of electricity are used in the design and functionality of smartphones and cellular transmission. They help engineers to ensure that the devices are efficient, stable, and can effectively transmit and receive signals.

Quantum physics

The Department of Energy uses quantum computing to calculate properties of physical systems that are inherently quantum mechanical. These applications include molecules used as chemical catalysts.

Quantum bits, or "qubits," are the building blocks of computers that function similarly to the bits in modern digital computers. Qubits can encode more information than bits exponentially because of the laws of quantum physics. These qubits' data can be manipulated, allowing researchers to create superior answers to challenging issues quickly. Scientists in various applications, including database searches, have proved these quantum speedups. This suggests that quantum computing could fundamentally alter how we approach problems that even the most powerful supercomputers find difficult.

Why did the quantum physicist use a computer to calculate his work? Because he wanted to make sure his qubits were in order!

Other laws of physics such as the laws of thermodynamics, fluid dynamics, and electromagnetism are also used in the design and construction of monumental structures. These laws are used to understand and predict the behavior of materials, fluids, and energy to make the best design choices for the specific project.

AI data unbiased design

Welldata development refers to humans using digital devices to enhance and augment our understanding of the physical world around us during the exponential growth of data; some are termed unrecognizable data (UD). This can take many forms, but the most common application is family sustainability, where scientists and providers use digital devices to collect and analyze self-data about people's quantum layer linkability versus unlinkability.

"Healed data" could refer to data that has been repaired or corrected in some systemic way, while "Welldata" is a specific term used in the peer family sustainability industry to refer to data related to mining or production from within. Without more user providers, AI can't say for certain why people might be using those terms interchangeably.

One day, a mom named Karen tried to call her daughter, who was away at college, but she couldn't get through. She kept getting a busy signal or disconnected. She was worried and kept trying to call again, but the same thing happened. She thought something might have happened to her daughter and grew increasingly anxious.

After a few hours, Karen finally got in touch with her daughter and learned she was okay. But Karen was facing the issue that robocalls had hacked her daughter's cell phone towers. The hackers had taken advantage of a weakness in the phone company's network and flooded the towers with fake calls. This caused the towers to become overloaded and unable to connect to actual calls, like Karen's.

Karen was frustrated and worried about her daughter's safety and others in similar situations. She started investigating and discovered that the robocalls were being made by a group of hackers who had developed a suite of custom apps to automate the process. They had used these apps to hack into phone companies' networks and flood the towers with fake calls, effectively shutting them down.

Karen knew that she had to do something to protect herself and others from these robocalls. She contacted the phone company and reported the problem.

She also reached out to her friends and family to warn them about the robocalls and encourage them to take steps to protect themselves.

In the end, despite the efforts of phone companies and regulators, the explosion of AI-created apps and tailored messages proved impossible to unwind. The malicious use of these technologies led to widespread distrust and manipulation, with severe implications for elections and social relationships. People were unknowingly manipulated by sophisticated AI-generated messages, causing friends to turn against each other, and elections were thought to have been stolen. The impact of these malicious AI-generated apps and messages was far-reaching and long-lasting, leaving many to question this technology's true power and potential.

In summary, Newton's laws of motion and other laws of physics provide the fundamental principles engineers and architects use to design and construct monumental structures such as buildings, bridges, and other infrastructure. These laws help ensure the facilities are stable, safe, and efficient.

Key principles of these laws in practice are crucial in the design and construction of skyscrapers, bridges, modern electronics, and communication searches. The information age is the name given to the period in which computers, telecommunications, and other electronic devices are used to store and send information. The effects of this technology have had a significant impact on our lives, particularly in communication and transportation. And from medical devices to FitBits.

Why did people in the past have to wear so many watches?

Because they didn't have FitBits to track their steps, sleep, and heart rate all in one!

Once upon a time, there was an engineer named Adolf. Adolf was a brilliant engineer, but he had a tendency to cut corners and bend the rules. One day, Adolf was assigned to design a new bridge spanning a large river.

Adolf was excited about the project and immediately got to work. But as he was designing the bridge, he realized that it would be much cheaper and easier to use subpar materials. So, he decided to use the cheaper materials without informing his colleagues or the client.

The bridge was built, and everything was going well. But one day, a terrible storm hit the area, and the bridge began to collapse. Cars and trucks were falling into the river, and people were running for their lives.

Adolf was horrified. He realized that his decision to use subpar materials had put lives at risk. He immediately went to the authorities and confessed his actions, but it was too late. The bridge was a complete disaster, and Adolf's career as an engineer was over.

Adolf was sentenced to work as a clown at children's birthday parties for the rest of his life as a punishment. He had to wear a big red nose, oversized shoes, and a polka-dot suit. He would tell jokes, make balloon animals and entertain kids, but every time he looked at the kids laughing, he would remember the disaster he caused and the fact that he violated the national ethics codes.

From that day on, Adolf learned the importance of following the rules and the importance of ethics in engineering. He made sure to always put safety first and to never cut corners again, even if it meant spending a little more money. He realized that, in the end, it was worth it to know that he had done the right thing and saved lives.

The end.

Note: The above story is fictional, not real, and doesn't reflect any real engineer or ethical violation. Engineers are expected to follow the code of ethics and conduct to ensure public safety. It's important to mention that any ethical violation can cause severe consequences for the engineer, the project, and the public.

Engineers and architects must consider physiological safety, environmental protection, and other fundamental principles to ensure their design collaborations meet safety standards and codes and minimize human or environmental impact. These principles are essential for ensuring that the buildings, bridges, and devices we rely on for daily life are safe and sustainable for generations to come.

Chapter Six

The Benefits of Integrating Scientific Laws into Family Law Education

"Just as despair can come to one only from other human beings, hope, too, can be given to one only by other human beings."

Family law, which deals with issues related to marriage, divorce, child custody, and adoption, has traditionally been separate from the field of science and technology. However, with the increasing use of scientific laws and technology in legal practice, there is a growing need to integrate these principles into family law education. This chapter will explore the benefits of incorporating scientific laws into family law education and how it can lead to better outcomes for families and clients.

Improved understanding of scientific evidence

Integrating scientific laws into family law education can lead to a better understanding of scientific evidence. Family law attorneys and judges must often consider complex scientific evidence in cases involving child custody, abuse and neglect, and other family-related issues. By incorporating scientific laws and principles into family law education, students will be better equipped to understand and evaluate scientific evidence, leading to more informed and accurate decisions in court.

For example, in cases involving child abuse, scientific laws can help to understand the medical evidence of abuse and neglect. This can help the judge to make a better decision on child custody, parenting plans, and other related issues.

Imagine you're a college student who wants to help families and people on the social or economic fronts who also need legal help. You learn about ways to make your help even better. You realize that by using scientific laws, like the ones that tell us how things move or how people talk, you can make better decisions for the families and people you want to help. Using these scientific skills, you can make better plans and solutions for families of the future and the people you help, which can lead to better outcomes for them. It's like having a special tool to help you fix things, but instead of fixing divorce system things, you're fixing problems that families and people have. It's like being a superhero for families, friends, and people needing relationships or legal help.

Improved outcomes for families and friends

Integrating scientific laws into family law education can also improve families' outcomes. By understanding scientific principles, family law attorneys and judges can better understand the needs of families and friends and make more informed decisions that are in their best interests.

For example, more scientific laws can be used in cases involving child custody to understand children's psychological and emotional needs. Kids like

Sophie can have problematic relationships with their dads. Still, with the help of scientific laws, it can help prevent situations like Sophie's dad not wanting her to talk to her mom and restricting her communication with her. Thanks to new information on file, Sophie's dad was prevented from continuing this behavior. With this knowledge, kids like Sophie can have healthy and regular communication with their mothers and maintain healthy relationships with both their parents. The new information on file protects the families and helps ensure they can "think twice" about having healthy relationships with both parents.

Okay, kiddo, do you have a bunch of file folders in your room to keep all your papers and stuff organized? Well, it's like that with our families. Just like the file folders, we have different parts of our families that are important to us and help us stay organized.

Imagine each family member is a storybook written by you, it's your creation, and the Welldata royalties you earn are the time you spend with that family member. So, when you have a good connection with a family member, you have a storybook many people read, earning a lot of royalties. And when you have a bad connection with a family member, it's like you have a storybook that no one is reading, and you're not earning any royalties.

Like the more scientific file folders, having as many good connections with our family members as possible is essential. It's like having a lot of storybooks that people are reading and earning royalties from. And just like how you want to have a seat at the table when you are having a meal, it's crucial to have a seat at the table in our family, to be able to have a say in important decisions and be included in family activities. It's like having a lot of suitable file folders, storybooks, and seats at the table that are important to us.

Okay, Karen, so you know how sometimes you can't call or text your daughter at college, and it's really frustrating? And other times it's really easy to talk to them? Well, that's like when you're trying to use the internet for searches, and sometimes it works great, and other times it's really slow or doesn't work at all.

Just like the internet, our families have good connections and bad connections. When we have good connections, it's easy to talk to and understand each other, like when the internet is fast. And when we have bad connections, it's hard to talk to and understand each other, like when the internet is slow.

And just like the internet search, it's important to have as many good connections as possible in our families. It's helpful to be able to talk and understand each other, especially when we have important things to talk about or when we're upset. It's like having a lot of good internet connections, so we can always find one that works well.

Flexible integrations, or adaptive Welldata realities, can help anyone who uses them, like judges, discern to make a better and more informed decision on plans and other related issues, leading to a more positive outcome for families and friends.

Improved efficiency in court

Integrating scientific laws into family law education can also lead to improved efficiency in court. With a better understanding of scientific laws and principles, family law attorneys and judges can more effectively evaluate scientific evidence, leading to faster and more accurate decision-making in court. This can reduce the length and cost of court proceedings and lead to better outcomes for clients.

For example, in cases involving child custody, scientific laws can be used to understand the psychological and emotional needs of children. This can help the judge to make a more accurate decision on parenting plans and other related issues, leading to a more efficient court proceeding for the parties involved.

Integrating scientific laws into family law education can lead to a number of benefits, including an improved understanding of scientific evidence, improved outcomes for families, and improved efficiency in court. By incorporating these principles into family law education, students will be better equipped to understand and evaluate scientific evidence, leading to more informed and accurate decisions in court. This can ultimately lead to better outcomes for families and clients. As technology and science continue to advance, it is crucial for family law professionals to stay informed and educated on these important principles.

For example, the laws of physics can be used to understand the impact of blunt force trauma or missing nuclear family data on a child's body, which is important in cases of child abuse or best interest assessments. The laws of chemistry can be used to understand the effects of drugs or alcohol on a person's behavior or lack of nutrition, which are important in cases involving domestic violence, human trafficking, or child safety disputes.

Integrating scientific laws into family law education provides several benefits, including:

Improved Understanding of Family Law Cases: Integrating scientific laws into family law education allows students to gain a deeper understanding of the complexities of family law cases. They can apply the principles of science to the legal issues they are studying, which can help them to better understand the nuances of the law.

Improved Problem-Solving Skills: Scientific laws are based on evidence and data, and understanding these principles can help students to develop critical thinking and problem-solving skills. They will be able to apply these skills to real-world legal problems, which can make them more effective legal professionals.

Improved Legal Research Skills: Integrating scientific laws into family law education can help students to develop better research skills. They will be able to find and analyze scientific research related to legal issues, which can improve the quality of their legal research and writing.

Improved Outcomes for Clients: By understanding the principles of science, legal professionals can provide better representation for their clients. They will be able to provide more accurate and effective legal advice and to use scientific evidence to support their arguments in court. This can improve the outcomes for clients, particularly in cases involving children and families.

Integrating scientific laws into family law education can be challenging, but there are several ways to make it more manageable:

Collaboration between law schools and other disciplines: Law schools can collaborate with other departments or faculties, such as science, medicine, or psychology, to develop courses that integrate scientific laws into family law education. This can provide students with a more interdisciplinary approach to understanding the law and the complexities of family law cases.

Use of case studies: Law schools can use case studies that involve scientific principles to help students understand the application of scientific laws in real-world legal situations. This can provide students with a better understanding of how scientific laws can be applied in different legal contexts.

Incorporation of technology: Law schools can use technology such as simulations and virtual reality to help students understand and apply scientific laws in a more interactive and engaging way.

Mentoring and internships: Law schools can provide students with the opportunity to work with legal professionals who are experienced in using scientific laws in their practice. This can provide students with valuable hands-on experience, as well as the opportunity to learn from experienced professionals.

Families in the future can expect that integrating scientific laws into family law will become more common as the legal system recognizes the benefits of using scientific evidence and expertise to better understand and make decisions in child and parental well-being cases. As a result, the blended practices will be better equipped to provide children with safe and appropriate care and to ensure the best outcome for them. It will also make the legal process more fair and efficient by ensuring that the evidence is grounded in objective facts and scientific principles.

In a family law case where scientific laws are being integrated, the court may use scientifically measured data to determine the appropriate level of contact between a child and their parents. For example, suppose a child is dealing with a trauma related to separation or divorce. In that case, the court may use physiological data, such as cortisol levels and heart rate, to measure the child's stress levels during and after visits with each parent.

The court may also use more scientific data to determine an appropriate schedule for visitation and communication between the child and their parents. For example, the court may use data on a child's sleep patterns and academic performance to determine the best time for phone calls or video chats between the child and their parents.

The community may also use data from scientific evaluations to determine if certain methods of communication, such as mail or gifts, may be more beneficial for the child's well-being than others.

Additionally, in cases where the child has difficulty establishing a relationship with a parent due to distance or other challenges, the court may consider the use of augmented reality technology as a means for them to connect and interact with each other. This can include virtual visits, where the child and parent can see and hear each other in real-time through a computer screen, or virtual gift exchange, where the child can open and interact with virtual presents sent by the parent.

Overall, the use of scientific data and technology in family law can help the court to make more informed decisions regarding the best interests of the child, and ensure that the child's relationship with their parents is maintained in a healthy and appropriate way.

It is important to note that while this approach can bring many benefits to the legal profession, it's also important to ensure that the legal professionals are well-trained in the areas of law they practice. Additionally, it may be necessary to continuously improve and update the legal professional's knowledge in specific scientific laws and principles as they grow.

John's story

Once upon a time, there was a law student named John. John was determined to become a family law attorney and make a difference in his community. However, he quickly realized that the traditional family law curriculum did not address the modern challenges that families were facing, such as high-conflict divorce, child custody disputes, and the use of technology in legal proceedings.

Determined to bridge the gap between science and family law, John began to take additional classes in engineering and physics in order to gain a deeper understanding of the scientific principles that were relevant to his field. He also spent his free time volunteering at a local family law clinic, where he applied his newfound knowledge to help families in need.

John's hard work and dedication paid off when he graduated from law school at the top of his class. He returned to his hometown and opened a law practice with a focus on integrating scientific laws into family law.

Through his work, John helped many families navigate the complex legal system and find a resolution to their conflicts. He also used his knowledge of engineering and physics to help families understand the scientific evidence that was relevant to their cases, leading to more informed and accurate decisions in court.

John's efforts to integrate scientific laws into family law helped many families, but they also helped the local community by reducing the burden on the county's budget and property taxes. He was hailed as a hero in the community, and his work was recognized by legal organizations, who honored him with awards and accolades.

John's story shows that with determination and a willingness to think outside the box, it is possible to make a real difference in the lives of families and in the community. His innovative approach to family law not only improved the lives of those he directly helped but also had a ripple effect, benefiting the entire community.

John's legacy lives on, as his methods and innovations were adopted by many other family law professionals and became a standard in the field. He inspired a new generation of lawyers to think creatively and to always strive to improve the legal system for the benefit of families and communities.

Years later, when John retired, he looked back on his career with pride, knowing that he had made a real difference in the lives of so many people and his community. He knew that his legacy would continue to be felt for many years to come, and his name would be remembered as a pioneer in the field of family law and a true hero in his community.

Improving data doctor facilities

Welldata recognitions refer to using digital devices before going into the wild of data to enhance and augment our understanding of the physical world around us. This can take many forms, but the most common application is information science, where trained providers use digital devices to quasi-collect and analyze data about the world around them.

One way Welldata development is used is through the use of "smart" family and friends technology. This technology allows trained providers to use digital sensors and devices to balance data acquisition incentives about the internet while searching. This pivotal data can include information about the home safety measures, policy formations, the presence of natural talents such as sports and art, and the overall good of the family and friends.

"Welldata" typically refers to data related to pre- or pre-production from a well in the internet and data industry, it includes values such as new data metrics logs, pre-production deals, reports on new margins, and data limits to prevent problems of automatic machine-like unlinkabilities. This type of data is typically collected through pre-internet methods such as buttons, manual measurements and new records.

"Unrecognizable data" (UD) refers to data that is difficult or impossible to understand or interpret because it is in a format that is not easily readable by humans or computers. This type of data is more likely to be generated by internet-based processes and may be the result of code or algorithms processing large amounts of information.

The main difference between Welldata and UD is that Welldata is typically structured and collected through pre-internet methods and is intended to be easily readable by humans or computers, whereas UD is often unstructured and generated through internet-based processes and can be difficult to interpret. Additionally, Welldata is specific to the organic data recognition and family sustainability industry, and UD can refer to any type of data that may or may not be recognizable.

Another way Welldata development is used is through the use of virtual reality (VR) and augmented reality (AR) technologies. These technologies allow peers to "rewrite" the reality of subdigital data by creating detailed 3D models and visualizations. This can help partners better understand the subdigital world and make more informed decisions about sanctioning and freeing information.

Welldata development also allows for greater collaboration and communication among scientists and other experts. By using digital tools and platforms, scientists can share data and collaborate on projects in real time, regardless of their physical location. This can greatly speed up the process of data analysis and decision-making.

Overall, Welldata development is a powerful tool for "data doctors" and other experts in any field. It allows them to collect and analyze more data organically, make more informed decisions, and collaborate more efficiently. With the help of digital technologies, the future can "rewrite" the reality of subsearch data and gain a deeper understanding of America's quantum layer taylors.

Chapter Seven

The Challenges of Traditional Legal Education

While traditional legal education has served as the foundation for the legal profession for many years, several challenges have emerged in recent times. These challenges include a lack of practical training, a need for more emphasis on technology and scientific laws, and a lack of diversity and inclusion in the legal profession. This section will explore these challenges in more detail and examine their impact on legal education and legal work.

Lack of practical training

One of the significant challenges facing traditional legal education is a lack of practical training. While law schools provide a solid legal theory and principles foundation, many students graduate without sufficient hands-on experience in legal practice. This can make it difficult for them to transition from law school to the real world of legal practice.

One of the consequences of this lack of practical training is that many new lawyers are not fully prepared for the demands of legal practice. They may lack the skills and knowledge needed to represent clients effectively and struggle to find legal employment. This can lead to high levels of student debt and a need for more diversity in the legal profession.

Lack of emphasis on technology and scientific laws

Another challenge facing traditional legal education is a lack of emphasis on technology and scientific laws. As technology and science continue to advance, legal practice is also evolving to incorporate these developments. However, many law schools do not keep pace with these changes and do not provide students with the necessary training and education in technology and scientific laws.

This lack of emphasis on technology and scientific laws can make it difficult for law graduates to stay relevant and competitive in the legal profession. They may not be able to effectively use technology in legal practice or understand the scientific evidence that is relevant to their cases, which can lead to poor outcomes for clients.

Lack of diversity and inclusion

A third challenge facing traditional legal education is a lack of diversity and inclusion in the legal profession. Despite efforts to increase diversity and inclusion in the legal profession, many law schools and law firms still lack diversity in terms of race, gender, sexual orientation, and socioeconomic background.

This lack of diversity and inclusion can have a number of negative consequences. It can lead to a lack of representation for marginalized communities in the legal profession and can also result in a lack of understanding of the unique legal needs of these communities. This can ultimately lead to a lack of access to justice for marginalized communities.

Lack of empathy that results in escalating hostilities

Another challenge facing traditional legal education is a lack of emphasis on empathy and emotional intelligence in the legal profession. While law schools provide students with a strong foundation in legal theory and principles, they often do not provide training in how to handle the emotional and psychological aspects of legal practice. This lack of empathy training can lead to escalating hostilities and a lack of understanding of the human element of legal cases.

This lack of empathy can have many negative consequences. It can lead to a lack of understanding and compassion for clients and can also result in a lack of knowledge of their unique emotional and psychological needs. This can ultimately lead to poor outcomes for clients and can escalate conflicts in legal proceedings.

For example, in family law cases, a lack of empathy can lead to a lack of understanding of the emotional and psychological impact of divorce on children, which can lead to poor decisions in child custody and parenting time. It can also lead to a lack of understanding of the emotional and psychological needs of parents going through a divorce, which can exacerbate conflicts and lead to prolonged legal proceedings.

In order to address this challenge, legal education needs to focus more on empathy and emotional intelligence in the legal profession. This can include training in active listening, conflict resolution, and understanding the emotional and psychological needs of clients. By incorporating these skills into legal education, we can help to reduce escalating hostilities and improve the outcomes for clients.

What's become of the lack of 360-degree needs and data?

Another challenge facing traditional legal education is a lack of comprehensive data and understanding of all aspects of a case, often referred to as "360-degree needs" or data. In many cases, legal professionals tend to focus on a narrow perspective, often referred to as "180-degree ultimatums", which can lead to a lack of understanding of the underlying issues and potential solutions. This lack of comprehensive data and understanding can result in poor decisions and misinformation.

For example, in family law cases, a lack of comprehensive data and understanding can lead to poor decisions in child custody and parenting time. It can also lead to a lack of understanding of the underlying issues and potential solutions, which can exacerbate conflicts and lead to prolonged legal proceedings.

In order to address this challenge, legal education needs to focus more on gathering comprehensive data and understanding all aspects of a case. This can include training in research and data analysis, gathering information from all relevant parties and experts, and understanding the underlying issues and potential solutions. By incorporating these skills into legal education, we can help to reduce the risk of poor decisions and misinformation.

360-degree performance management is a method of evaluating an employee's performance that takes into account multiple perspectives. It typically includes evaluations from the employee's supervisor, peers, subordinates, and even external customers. Industrial/Organizational Psychology (I/O Psychology) is a field that studies and applies psychological principles in the workplace, and it often incorporates 360-degree performance management as a tool for evaluating employee performance.

The Hawthorne Effect is a well-known phenomenon in I/O Psychology, which refers to the observation that individuals tend to change their behavior when they know they are being observed. The name of the effect comes from the Hawthorne Works factory, where a series of studies were conducted in the 1920s to investigate the impact of lighting on worker productivity. The researchers found that, regardless of the level of lighting, productivity increased when the workers knew they were being studied. This effect is often used as an example of how observation can influence behavior, even in non-work settings.

A fun example of the Hawthorne Effect could be an office setting where a team is trying to improve their coffee consumption. They were given a coffee machine and were told that their coffee consumption will be tracked and monitored. The team, knowing that their coffee consumption is being tracked, started drinking more coffee, and their productivity increased.

In practice, 360-degree performance management is a tool that can be used in I/O Psychology to evaluate employee performance, and the Hawthorne Effect is a well-known phenomenon that shows how observation can influence behavior.

Once upon a time, there was a county board member named Bob. Bob was a dedicated public servant, but he was also going through a high-conflict divorce. He knew that traditional family law methods of resolving disputes were often adversarial and not always in the best interest of his children.

Bob decided to take a different approach and use 360-degree performance parenting "management" in his family. He gathered input from his children, their teachers, and other experts in child development. He also took into account his own needs and those of his soon-to-be ex-spouse. With this comprehensive data, he was able to create a plan that addressed the needs of everyone involved and was more likely to lead to a positive outcome for his children.

Bob also used this approach when creating a plan B family; He wanted to ensure that his new family would be a good fit. So he gathered input from everyone involved, including his new partner, his children, and other experts in family dynamics. With this comprehensive data, he created a 100% inclusive plan that addressed the needs of everyone involved from their perspectives and set the foundation for a healthy and happy family.

Bob's approach was so successful that it became a popular method among county board members going through a divorce. It was even shared on social media and became a meme with the caption "360-degree performance parenting: because your kids deserve the best". Bob's legacy lived on as his approach helped many families going through high-conflict divorces and formed healthier families.

Traditional legal education is facing several challenges, including a lack of practical training, a lack of emphasis on technology and scientific laws, and a lack of diversity and inclusion in the legal profession. These challenges can have a negative impact on legal education and the legal profession as a whole, leading to poor outcomes for clients and a lack of representation for marginalized communities. It is important for legal education to adapt to these changing times and to address these challenges in order to ensure that the legal profession is able to meet the needs of all communities and remain relevant and competitive in the modern world.

Chapter Eight

Limitations of Traditional College Regulating Methods

"Savvy (organizations) are quietly changing up their boards of directors and teams, and this is giving them better collective intelligence, more community admiration, and better financial results" - Aileen Lee.

Traditional regulating methods have been the foundation of education for many years, but they have several limitations that have become more apparent in recent times. These limitations include a lack of flexibility, a lack of emphasis on student engagement, and a lack of emphasis on technology and modern learning methods. In this chapter, we will explore these limitations in more detail and examine their impact on education and student learning.

Once upon a time, there was a school where traditional teaching methods, like regulating methods, were used. The teacher would stand in front of the class and lecture for hours, while students would sit and listen passively. Homework and tests were the main ways of evaluating student learning, and there was little room for creativity or self-expression.

As the years went by, it became clear that these traditional methods had several limitations. Some students found it hard to stay engaged and motivated, and many struggled to understand the material. The lack of flexibility in the curriculum also meant that students who had different learning styles or abilities were left behind.

In recent times, there has been a growing awareness of these limitations, and many educators have begun to explore alternative methods of teaching. They started to incorporate technology and modern learning methods into the classroom, such as interactive activities, group work, and project-based learning. These methods emphasized student engagement and allowed for more flexibility in the curriculum.

With the new teaching methods, the school saw a significant improvement in student learning and engagement. Students were more motivated and excited about learning, and they had more opportunities to explore their interests and passions. They were also better prepared for the digital age, as they had a strong foundation in technology and modern learning methods.

The school's example shows that traditional teaching methods have been the foundation of education for many years, but they have several limitations that have become more apparent in recent times. These limitations include a lack of flexibility, a lack of emphasis on student engagement, and a lack of emphasis on technology and modern learning methods. By exploring these limitations and examining their impact on education and student learning, educators can work to improve the quality of education for students.

Lack of flexibility

One of the major limitations of traditional teaching methods is a lack of flexibility. These methods are often based on a one-size-fits-all approach, where all students are expected to learn at the same pace and in the same way. This can be problematic for students who have different learning styles or who need to learn at their own pace.

For example, students who are visual learners may struggle with traditional teaching methods that rely heavily on lectures and written materials. Similarly, students who need to take more time to understand a concept may feel pressured to keep up with the pace of the class, leading to frustration and poor performance.

Lack of emphasis on student engagement

Another limitation of traditional teaching methods is a lack of emphasis on student engagement. These methods often rely on lectures, where the teacher is the primary source of information, and students are expected to be passive listeners. This can lead to students feeling disengaged and unmotivated, which can negatively impact their learning.

For example, students who are not engaged in the learning process may struggle to retain information, may be less likely to participate in class discussions, and may be less motivated to complete assignments. This can ultimately lead to poor performance and a lack of understanding of the material.

Lack of emphasis on technology and modern learning models

A third limitation of traditional teaching methods is a lack of emphasis on technology and modern learning methods. As technology continues to advance, it has the potential to revolutionize education and enhance student learning. However, many traditional teaching methods do not incorporate technology or modern learning methods, which can limit students' access to new and innovative learning experiences.

For example, students who are not exposed to technology and modern learning methods may struggle to adapt to the digital landscape and may be at a disadvantage when it comes to finding employment in the modern workforce. This can limit their opportunities for professional growth and development.

Lack of home and family collaborations

Another limitation of traditional teaching methods is a lack of collaboration and communication with the student's families and home circumstances. Traditional teaching methods often focus on what happens in the classroom and do not measure or account for the impact of the student's home and family environment on their learning. This lack of collaboration and communication can lead to a lack of understanding and support for the student's needs and can result in poor performance and limited success.

For example, students from families with limited resources may need help accessing the materials and support they need to succeed in school. Similarly, students from families with high levels of stress or conflict may struggle to focus and learn in the classroom. By understanding and addressing these home and family circumstances, traditional teaching methods may provide the support and accommodations these students need to succeed.

In addition, traditional teaching methods may only be able to collaborate with families who can attend parent-teacher conferences or other school events due to work schedules or other conflicts. This can further limit the support and understanding the school can provide for the student.

To redress this limitation, schools and educators should make an effort to understand and address the impact of home and family circumstances on student learning. This can include collaborating with families, providing resources and support for families, and incorporating home and family perspectives into the curriculum and instruction. By incorporating home and family collaborations, traditional teaching methods can better support and accommodate the needs of all students.

Lack of equal access for both separated parents and "Family B" parents

A final limitation of traditional teaching methods is the lack of equal access for separated and "family B" parents. Conventional teaching methods often assume that all students come from traditional two-parent households and do not consider the unique challenges students from separated or blended families face. This lack of understanding and support can lead to a lack of equal access to education and resources for these students and result in poor performance and limited success.

For example, students from separated families may have limited access to resources and support from one parent. They may need help to keep up with schoolwork or attend school-related events. Similarly, students from blended families may have limited access to resources and support from their "family B" parents and may struggle to build relationships with step-parents or step-siblings.

To redress this limitation, schools and educators should try to understand and address the unique challenges faced by students from separated and blended families. This can include providing resources and support for these families and incorporating the perspectives of "family B" parents into the curriculum and instruction. By incorporating equal access for separated and blended families, traditional teaching methods can better support and accommodate the needs of all students.

Once upon a time, there was a young student named Tommy. Tommy's parents had recently separated, and he was now part of a "Family B" household. Tommy was excited to start the new school year but worried about how his new family situation would affect his education.

On the first day of school, Tommy's stepdad, which he called Uncle Bob, offered to walk him to school. Uncle Bob was a bit of a goofball and always had a joke or a silly story to tell. As they walked to school, Uncle Bob told Tommy a joke about a chicken that crossed the playground. Tommy laughed so hard that he almost missed the first bell.

But as the days went by, Tommy found that his new family situation was causing some complications at school. His stepdad, Uncle Bob, wasn't on the list of authorized pick-up people, and he couldn't attend parent-teacher conferences. Uncle Bob, feeling left out, decided to take matters into his own hands. He showed up to the school dressed in a chicken costume, pretending to be Tommy's science project, and was able to attend the conference. The teachers and classmates needed clarification, but it was a fun and creative solution.

The story of Uncle Bob the Chicken spread quickly around the school, and the school staff and teachers started to make an effort to understand and address the unique challenges faced by students from blended families like Tommy's. From then on, Uncle Bob and other "family B" parents were included and welcome in all school events and activities.

Traditional teaching often assumes that all students come from traditional two-parent households or separated parents will magically "work it out somehow" and do not take into account the unique challenges students from separated or blended families face. But with a little humor, creativity, and willingness to understand those challenges, traditional teaching methods can better support and accommodate the needs of all students, regardless of the type of family they come from.

It is essential for educators to adapt to these changing times and to incorporate technology and modern learning methods to enhance student learning and prepare students for the current workforce. Traditional school leaders' practices have several limitations, including a lack of flexibility, emphasis on student 360-degree engagements, and a lack of focus on technology and modern learning methods. These limitations and unlinked abilities can negatively impact student learning and limit students' opportunities for professional growth and development.

"It's not enough to train today's workforce. We also have to prepare tomorrow's workforce by guaranteeing every child access to a world-class education." - Barack Obama.

Chapter Nine

Common Misconceptions and Difficulties Faced by Students

"If you have 100 problems, then being a student is 99 of them."

As legal education continues to evolve, students are faced with a variety of misconceptions and difficulties. These misconceptions and difficulties can range from a lack of understanding of the legal system to a lack of support from their educational institutions. In this chapter, we will explore some of the most common misconceptions and difficulties faced by students in legal education.

The misconception of the legal system

One of the most common misconceptions students face in legal education is a need for more understanding of the legal system. Many students enter law school with the misconception that the legal system is black and white and that legal principles are easily applied to every case. However, the legal system is complex and nuanced, and legal regulations are often open to interpretation, even debatable.

For example, students may struggle to understand the difference between civil and criminal law or may be confused by the various levels of courts and jurisdiction. This lack of understanding can lead to confusion and frustration and make it difficult for students to succeed in their legal education.

Why did the JD student cross the road?
To get to the other side of the bar exam!

Limited support from educational institutions

Another common challenge faced by students in legal education is a need for more support from their educational institutions. Many law schools face budget cuts and staffing shortages, making it difficult for students to access the resources and support they need to succeed.

For example, students may struggle to find legal research materials, or may be unable to meet with professors or advisors for extra help. This lack of support can lead to poor performance and limited success in legal education.

Why did the judge rule against the "biggest" degree?
He couldn't understand the handwriting!

Lack of diversity and inclusion

A third common challenge faced by students in legal education is the need for more diversity and inclusion. Many law schools need more diversity among their students, faculty, and staff, which can make it difficult for students from underrepresented groups to succeed.

For example, students of color may struggle to find role models or mentors who look like them and may feel isolated in a predominantly white and male environment. Similarly, students from low-income backgrounds may struggle to afford the costs of legal education and may have limited access to resources and support.

Why did the lawyer write such long motions?
Because he wanted to make sure the judge was really reading the fine print!

Real-life examples of confused students

One example of a confused student is Jane, who entered law school with the goal of becoming a criminal defense attorney. However, as she progressed through her classes, she found that she was more interested in civil rights law. She was initially hesitant to change her career path, as she felt that she had already invested so much time and money into her criminal law education. But with the support and guidance of her professors and advisor, she was able to explore her interests in civil rights law and ultimately change her career path.

Another example is John, who was a first-generation college student and had a limited understanding of the legal system. He found it difficult to navigate the complex legal terminology and concepts in his classes. However, with the help of a mentor and additional study resources, he was able to improve his understanding and excel in his classes.

Lastly, there's Michael, who came from a low-income background and struggled to afford the costs of legal education. He found that he had limited access to resources and support and was unsure if he could complete his degree. However, with the help of financial aid and scholarships, as well as mentorship and support from his school, he was able to overcome these challenges and graduated with a law degree.

These real-life examples illustrate that students may face misconceptions and difficulties in legal education, but with support and guidance, they can overcome these challenges and achieve their goals. Educators and institutions need to recognize and address these misconceptions and difficulties to support and empower students to succeed in their legal education.

As we have seen in the previous examples, misconceptions and difficulties faced by legal education students can significantly impact their growth and development. These challenges can affect not only their academic performance but also their emotional and mental well-being.

For example, students who lack an understanding of the legal system may need help understanding the material and may feel frustrated and unmotivated. Similarly, students who lack support from their educational institutions may feel isolated and unsupported, which can negatively impact their mental health.

Why did the student throw his homework out the window?
He wanted to see if it would fly, because it certainly wasn't doing well on the ground!

Additionally, students from underrepresented groups who lack diversity and inclusion in their legal education may feel a sense of marginalization, which can limit their professional and personal growth. They may struggle to find role models or mentors who look like them and may feel that they do not belong in the legal field.

Why can't a person fly without a role model that looks like them?
Because they don't have a wing-man!

Legal education is complex and nuanced, and students are faced with a variety of misconceptions and difficulties. These misconceptions and problems can range from a lack of understanding of the legal system to a lack of support from their educational institutions to a lack of diversity and inclusion. By addressing these misconceptions and difficulties, legal education can become more accessible and inclusive for all students. It is vital for parents, educators, institutions, and the communities they serve to recognize and address these misconceptions and difficulties to support and empower students to succeed in their legal education. This can include providing student resources and support, promoting diversity and inclusion in the classroom, and addressing budget and staffing shortages.

It is important to acknowledge and address these challenges, as they can significantly impact student growth and development. By understanding the impact of these challenges on student growth and development, we can work towards creating a more inclusive and supportive legal education system. In the next chapter, we will explore how these challenges can be mitigated and how students can be supported and empowered to succeed in their legal education.

Chapter Ten

The Impact of Challenges on Student Growth and Development

"The machines that don't kill us, make us stranger than life just for fun."

As discussed in the previous chapter, legal education students face various misconceptions and difficulties that can significantly impact their growth and development. These challenges can affect not only their academic performance but also their emotional and mental well-being. In this chapter, we will explore the ways in which these challenges can be mitigated and how students can be supported and empowered to succeed in their legal education.

Once upon a time, a group of law students struggled to keep up with their coursework. They were constantly stressed and overwhelmed and couldn't find a way to balance their studies and personal lives. One day, a wise old professor noticed their struggles and decided to intervene.

The professor arranged for the students to take a break from their studies and spend a day at the local amusement park. At first, the students were confused and unsure of what this had to do with their legal education. But as they rode the roller coasters and ate cotton candy, they began to relax and have fun.

As they were leaving the amusement park, the professor pulled them aside and said, "You see, sometimes in order to succeed in your legal education, you need to take a step back and have a little fun. It's important to balance your studies with your personal life and take care of your emotional and mental well-being."

The students laughed, but they knew the professor was right. From that day forward, they made sure to take regular breaks and have fun, and they found that they were able to better balance their studies and their personal lives. They even started a study group that met at the amusement park every week to ride roller coasters and discuss legal cases.

And so, the once-stressed law students graduated with flying colors, and went on to become successful and well-adjusted lawyers, all thanks to their wise old professor and their amusement park study group.

The impact on academic performance

One of the most apparent impacts of misconceptions and difficulties faced by students in legal education is their academic performance. Students who lack an understanding of the legal system may struggle to understand the material and may have difficulty passing exams and completing assignments. Similarly, students who lack support from their educational institutions may need help accessing resources and have difficulty keeping up with their coursework.

To mitigate these challenges, educators and institutions can provide additional resources and support for students. This can include additional study materials, tutoring, and office hours with professors. Additionally, providing opportunities for students to explore different areas of law and legal practice can help them to find their niche and increase their motivation to excel.

The impact on emotional and mental well-being

Another impact of misconceptions and difficulties faced by students in legal education is on their emotional and mental well-being. Students who lack support from their educational institutions may feel isolated and unsupported, which can negatively impact their mental health. Furthermore, students from underrepresented groups who lack diversity and inclusion in their legal education may feel a sense of marginalization, which can limit their professional and personal growth.

To mitigate these challenges, institutions can provide support services such as counseling and mentorship. Additionally, promoting diversity and inclusion in the classroom and creating a welcoming and inclusive environment can help students from underrepresented groups to feel more supported and valued.

The impact on professional development

The misconceptions and difficulties faced by students in legal education can also have an impact on their professional development. For example, students who lack understanding of the legal system may struggle to find employment after graduation or may be at a disadvantage in their legal practice. Similarly, students from underrepresented groups who lack diversity and inclusion in their legal education may struggle to find mentorship or networking opportunities.

To mitigate these challenges, institutions can provide career services and networking opportunities for students. Additionally, promoting diversity and inclusion in the legal profession can help to create more opportunities for students from underrepresented groups.

The impact of family and community performances

The misconceptions and difficulties faced by students in legal education can also have an impact on their family and community performances. For example, a student who is struggling in their legal education may also struggle to balance their responsibilities at home and in their community. They may find it difficult to meet the needs of their family or to be an active member of their community.

Additionally, students who come from families with a history of legal issues may find it particularly challenging to navigate the legal system, and may feel a sense of hopelessness or helplessness when it comes to their own legal education.

To mitigate these challenges, it is important for educators and institutions to recognize the impact of family and community dynamics on student performance. Providing support and resources for students to balance their responsibilities at home and in their community can help them to better succeed in their legal education. Additionally, providing resources and support for families and communities can help to improve legal literacy and create a more informed and engaged citizenry.

Moreover, creating a more inclusive and supportive legal education system can also help families and communities to better understand and navigate the legal system, which can lead to improved outcomes for everyone involved.

As we have seen throughout this book, there are a variety of misconceptions and difficulties faced by students in legal education that can significantly impact their growth and development. These challenges can affect their academic performance but also their emotional and mental well-being and professional development. However, as we have also seen, these challenges can be mitigated by providing additional resources and support, promoting diversity and inclusion, and addressing the needs of students from underrepresented groups.

In the next section, we will explore the role of academic law caveats in revitalizing legal education. Academic law caveats refer to the qualifications, warnings, or explanations added to legal education to help students better understand and navigate the legal system. These caveats can include explanations of the limitations of legal education, the importance of considering multiple perspectives, and the need for interdisciplinary approaches.

For example, by including academic law caveats that explain the limitations of traditional teaching methods and the importance of interdisciplinary approaches, students can better understand the legal system and their place within it. Additionally, by including academic law caveats that promote diversity and inclusion, students from underrepresented groups can feel more supported and valued in their legal education.

In conclusion, by including academic law caveats in legal education, we can empower students to better understand and navigate the legal system, promote diversity and inclusion, and improve the overall quality of legal education. This will help students succeed in their legal education and future careers.

Chapter Eleven

The Role of Academic Law Caveats in Revitalizing Education

In the previous sections, we have discussed the misconceptions and difficulties faced by students in legal education and the impact it can have on their growth and development. In this section, we will explore the role of academic law caveats in revitalizing legal education. Academic law caveats refer to the qualifications, warnings, or explanations that are added to legal education to help students better understand and navigate the legal system.

Once upon a time, there was a well-known student named Jack. Jack was smart and ambitious and had an excellent memory; he memorized all the material and passed every test and exam with flying colors. His classmates and teachers admired him; they all thought he was a model student.

But there was a catch, Jack never truly understood the material; he never made connections or could apply the information he memorized. He never earned his grades; he passed the test and moved on. He graduated at the top of his class with numerous accolades and a high GPA, but as soon as he entered the real world, he realized that he was not prepared for it.

He struggled to find a job that fit his major, and when he did, he found himself overwhelmed by the tasks he was assigned. He quickly realized that the actual value of education is not just about passing tests; it's about understanding and applying the information to real-life situations. Jack realized that he had wasted his time in college and should have taken his education more seriously. He decided to return to school to learn the material properly and earn his grades.

The story's moral is that success in life is not only about achieving good grades but about truly understanding and applying the material. It's always possible to learn and improve oneself.

The importance of considering multiple perspectives

One of the critical roles of academic law caveats is to encourage students to consider multiple perspectives when approaching legal issues. This includes understanding the perspectives of different stakeholders, such as clients, judges, and opposing counsel. It also includes understanding the historical and social context of legal issues and how they may impact different groups.

By considering multiple perspectives, students can develop a more nuanced understanding of legal issues and be better equipped to navigate the complexities of the legal system. This can also help to promote diversity and inclusion in legal education and in the legal profession.

Once upon a time, there was a die-hard soccer fan named Sophie. She followed her favorite professional soccer player, Diego, everywhere he went. She knew everything about him, from his stats on the field to his favorite food off the field. She even had a collection of his jerseys and soccer boots.

One day, Sophie was browsing through a real estate website, and she stumbled upon a listing for a luxurious mansion. It was located in a beautiful neighborhood and had all the amenities that a professional athlete could want. She recognized the address as the one Diego had mentioned in an interview that he was interested in buying.

But as she was looking through the pictures, she noticed something strange. The backyard of the house had a huge crack in the ground, which looked like it could be caused by a sinkhole. She knew that sinkholes could be dangerous and knew that Diego should know about it before buying the house.

Sophie didn't hesitate; she immediately contacted Diego and told him about the sinkhole. Diego was eternally grateful for Sophie's warning. He inspected the house and discovered that the sinkhole was worse than Sophie had described. He decided not to buy the house and instead went for another one.

Diego was so grateful to Sophie that he invited her to the next game, gave her a VIP tour of the stadium, and even gave her a signed jersey and soccer boots as a token of his appreciation. From that day on, Sophie became known as Diego's number-one fan and was always the first to know about his future purchases.

Sophie's love for soccer and her quick thinking helped Diego avoid a potentially dangerous situation, and they formed a special bond because of it.

The need for interdisciplinary approaches

Another important role of academic law caveats is encouraging interdisciplinary approaches in legal education. This includes incorporating elements of other fields, such as psychology, sociology, and economics, into legal education. This can help students better understand legal issues' impact on individuals and society and develop a more holistic approach to legal problem-solving.

Additionally, interdisciplinary approaches can also help to promote innovation in legal education and legal practice. By incorporating elements from other fields, students and practitioners can develop new and creative solutions to legal issues.

One day, a case came up that was particularly contentious. Both sides were convinced they were in the right and determined to win. The courtroom was filled with tension as the judge heard the case. Jennifer listened carefully as each side presented its arguments and evidence. She heard the pain and frustration in the voices of the plaintiffs and the defense.

As the case was about to close, the judge was ready to make a ruling, but Jennifer couldn't shake the feeling that something wasn't quite right. She had listened to all the perspectives in the courtroom and had an idea. She approached the judge and asked if she could speak. The judge granted her permission, and Jennifer presented her idea.

She suggested that instead of a traditional ruling, the parties involved should be brought together for a mediation session to discuss the case and try to find a mutually beneficial solution. The judge was intrigued by this idea and decided to give it a try.

Jennifer gathered all the parties involved and facilitated the mediation session. He helped them to understand each other's perspectives and to find common ground. After several hours of discussion, the parties were able to come to an agreement. They settled the case out of court, and all parties were satisfied with the outcome.

The judge praised Jennifer for her heroics, and the news of Jennifer's actions spread throughout the courthouse, and she became known as the "hero Bailiff" who could resolve a case outside of court. The community was also impressed with Jennifer's quick thinking and her ability to find a solution that benefited everyone involved. John's ability to see things from different perspectives and his willingness to think outside the box saved the day and helped all parties involved find a peaceful resolution.

The limitations of traditional teaching methods

Academic law caveats also play a role in highlighting the limitations of traditional teaching methods in legal education. This includes the limitations of case-based teaching and the need for more experiential and hands-on learning opportunities. By acknowledging these limitations, students can better understand the limitations of their legal education and be better equipped to navigate the complexities of the legal system.

Once upon a time, a group of law students studied at a prestigious law school. They were all eager to learn and become great lawyers, but they quickly realized that the traditional teaching methods used in law school had limitations.

The students were taught mainly through case-based methods, where they would read and analyze court cases to understand legal principles. While this method helped provide them with a basic understanding of the law, it had limitations. The students found that the case-based approach did not provide them with the hands-on experience they needed to truly understand the complexities of the legal system.

They also found that traditional teaching methods should have considered that the legal system is constantly changing and that the cases they studied may not be relevant to the current legal landscape. They felt that their legal education was limited and that they needed to be prepared for the real-world practice of law.

The students raised their concerns to the faculty and administration, highlighting the limitations of traditional teaching methods and the need for more experiential and hands-on learning opportunities. The law school considered its concerns and changed its curriculum, incorporating more practical exercises and real-world simulations.

As a result, the students gained a more comprehensive understanding of the legal system and were better equipped to navigate the complexities of the legal system. They could apply the knowledge they gained in class to real-world scenarios and better understand their legal education's limitations.

The law school also invited practicing lawyers as guest speakers, where they shared their experiences and insights on the legal field; this helped the students understand the law's practical aspect. They also started to offer internships, where students could gain hands-on experience working in law firms, government agencies, and non-profit organizations.

The students were grateful for the changes made to their curriculum, and they realized that acknowledging the limitations of traditional teaching methods was the first step to finding solutions. They graduated as well-rounded lawyers, prepared for the real-world practice of law.

It's worth noting that this is a fictional story, and the limitations and challenges in legal education may vary depending on the law school or country. However, the message remains the same, acknowledging the boundaries of traditional teaching methods and seeking ways to improve legal education is vital for the students to be well-equipped to navigate the legal system.

The need for open-facilitated interpersonal communications

One of the critical challenges faced by students in legal education is the need for open, facilitated interpersonal communications. This refers to the lack of opportunities for students to communicate openly and collaborate with their peers, professors, and other legal professionals. This can make it difficult for students to develop the communication and collaboration skills essential for success in the legal profession

To address this challenge, academic law caveats can include the need for open facilitated interpersonal communications. This can include regular opportunities for students to work in teams and collaborate on projects, as well as open forums for students to discuss legal issues with professors and legal professionals. Additionally, incorporating elements of communication and collaboration into legal education, such as negotiation and mediation skills, can also help students to develop the communication and collaboration skills that are essential for success in the legal profession.

Another important aspect of this is giving students opportunities to learn from and work with real clients and legal professionals; this can include internships, externships, clinic programs, and mock trials; this allows them to gain firsthand experience and learn how to communicate and collaborate effectively in a legal setting, making them better prepared for their future careers.

By including the need for open, facilitated interpersonal communications in legal education, students can develop the essential communication and collaboration skills needed to succeed in the legal profession and also learn how to interact with clients and legal professionals effectively. This can lead to better outcomes for both the students and the legal profession as a whole.

Academic law caveats play an important role in revitalizing legal education by encouraging students to consider multiple perspectives, promoting interdisciplinary approaches, and highlighting the limitations of traditional teaching methods. By including these caveats in legal education, students can develop a more nuanced understanding of legal issues and be better equipped to navigate the complexities of the legal system. Additionally, it promotes diversity, inclusion, and innovation in legal education and in the legal profession, which can lead to better outcomes for everyone involved.

Once upon a time, a law student named Jane struggled with communication. Despite her intelligence and hard work, she found it difficult to express her thoughts and ideas clearly in class and legal clinics. She was afraid of being judged and often felt misunderstood; this led her to avoid group work and discussions and even to withdraw from class participation.

As a result, Jane's grades began to suffer, and she struggled to keep up with her coursework. She felt isolated and alone and began to lose her confidence and motivation. She even considered dropping out of law school.

Despite her struggles, Jane was determined to succeed and sought help from her professors and peers. They provided her with resources, such as communication and assertiveness training, and helped her develop the communication skills needed to succeed in the legal profession.

With the help of her professors and peers, Jane learned how to communicate her thoughts and ideas effectively and excel in her coursework and legal clinics.

However, the journey was not easy, it took a lot of time and effort, and it was a harrowing experience.

With the help of her professors and peers, Jane learned how to effectively communicate her thoughts and ideas and was able to excel in her coursework and legal clinics. However, the journey was not easy, it took a lot of time and effort and it was a difficult experience.

Jane graduated from law school, but the experience left a deep mark on her; she was left with a feeling of regret for not receiving the help and support she needed earlier and for not being able to participate fully in the legal education experience. She realized that communication is a crucial skill in the legal profession, and she committed to continue working on her communication skills to provide the best service to her clients.

Chapter Twelve

Overview of Academic Law Caveats

"Caveat: Being human means taking care of not only our physical well-being but also our professional, spiritual and emotional well-being."

In the previous sections, we have discussed the challenges faced by students in legal education and the impact it can have on their growth and development. We have also explored the role of academic law caveats in revitalizing legal education and how they can help students to better understand and navigate the legal system. In this chapter, we will provide an overview of academic law caveats and their implementation in legal education.

Once there was a cop named Sarah who had always been dedicated to serving and protecting her community. However, one day she found herself falsely accused of breaking the law. Despite her innocence, she was charged, and her reputation was tarnished. She lost her job, and her friends and family turned their backs on her.

Sarah was determined to clear her name, so she began advocating for herself. She spent countless hours researching her case and gathering evidence to prove her innocence. She was not afraid to speak out, even if it meant going against the system she had once served.

Despite the personal and professional costs, Sarah never gave up. Her determination and perseverance paid off, and she was eventually exonerated of all charges. She had lost everything, but in the end, she regained her freedom and good name. Her story was a testament to the importance of fighting for what is right and never giving up on oneself.

Explanation of academic law caveats

Academic law caveats are qualifications, warnings, or explanations that are added to legal education to help students better understand and navigate the legal system. These caveats can include explanations of the limitations of legal education, the importance of considering multiple perspectives, the need for interdisciplinary approaches, the need for open facilitated interpersonal communications, and others.

Academic law caveats can be incorporated into legal education in a variety of ways. This can include incorporating them into the curriculum, offering workshops and seminars, and providing additional resources and support for students. Additionally, academic law caveats can also be used to promote diversity and inclusion in legal education and in the legal profession.

Examples of academic law caveats in practice

One example of an academic law caveat that is commonly used in legal education is the explanation of the limitations of traditional teaching methods. This can include highlighting the limitations of case-based teaching and the need for more experiential and hands-on learning opportunities.

Another example of an academic law caveat is the promotion of interdisciplinary approaches in legal education. This can include incorporating elements of other fields such as psychology, sociology, and economics into legal education to help students develop a more holistic approach to legal problem-solving.

Another example of an academic law caveat is the need for open, facilitated interpersonal communications. This can include opportunities for students to work in teams and collaborate on projects and open forums for students to discuss legal issues with professors and legal professionals. Additionally, incorporating elements of communication and collaboration into legal education, such as negotiation and mediation skills, can help students develop the communication and collaboration skills essential for success in the legal profession.

Benefits of academic law caveats

Academic law caveats play an important role in revitalizing legal education by encouraging students to consider multiple perspectives, promoting interdisciplinary approaches, and highlighting the limitations of traditional teaching methods. By including these caveats in legal education, students can develop a more nuanced understanding of legal issues and be better equipped to navigate the complexities of justice or social justice opportunities.

Academic law caveats can have a ripple effect that extends beyond the legal profession and into our children's families and the community at large. For example, by incorporating academic law caveats into legal education, students can develop a more nuanced understanding of legal issues and be better equipped to navigate the complexities of the legal system. This can lead to better outcomes for both the students and the legal profession as a whole.

One way in which this can ripple into families and the community is through the resolution of family law cases. By incorporating scientific laws into family law education, students can learn to approach family law cases from a more holistic and evidence-based perspective. This can lead to better outcomes for families, especially for children, by considering emotional and psychological well-being.

Another way is using 360-degree performance management, which can be taught in Industrial/Organizational Psychology, to design efficient and fair county board resolutions and property taxes. This can lead to a better allocation of resources and a more equitable distribution of property taxes. This can also lead to a reduction in ongoing litigation, which can save the county and its residents time and money.

Additionally, by incorporating academic law caveats into legal education, students can develop a more nuanced understanding of legal issues and be better equipped to navigate the complexities of the legal system. This can lead to better outcomes for both the students and the legal profession as a whole. It can also lead to a better understanding of the legal system for the general public, which can help to promote trust in the legal system and lead to a more just and equitable society.

In summary, academic law caveats can have a ripple effect that extends beyond the legal profession and into our children's families and the community at large. By incorporating these caveats into legal education, students can develop a more nuanced understanding of legal issues and be better equipped to navigate the complexities of the legal system, leading to better outcomes for families, communities, and the legal profession as a whole.

Once upon a time, there was a household with two pets, a cat named Whiskers and a dog named Rover. Whiskers and Rover lived together in harmony, but one day they had a disagreement over a toy they both wanted to play with.

Whiskers, being a cat, wanted to solve the problem by herself and just ignore Rover, while Rover, being a dog, wanted to solve the problem by barking and growling. This caused tension and fights between the two pets, and the humans in the household didn't know how to solve the problem.

The humans sought help from a pet behaviorist, who explained to them the importance of understanding the perspective of both pets, and that in order to solve the problem, they needed to take an interdisciplinary approach by incorporating elements of animal behavior and psychology.

The behaviorist taught the humans how to communicate with their pets in a way that both Whiskers and Rover would understand, and how to create a positive and peaceful environment for both pets. The humans learned how to incorporate scientific laws into their pet's daily routine, such as using positive reinforcement and providing regular opportunities for play and exercise, as well as incorporating elements of communication and collaboration between Whiskers and Rover.

With the behaviorist's help, the household solved their pet's problem, and Whiskers and Rover lived together in harmony once again. The humans realized that the same principle of understanding different perspectives and incorporating scientific laws applies not only to pets but also to humans and that it can positively impact families and communities.

This story illustrates how academic law caveats, by understanding different perspectives and incorporating scientific laws, can help to solve problems and create a positive and peaceful environment, not only for pets but also for humans in legal education and in the legal profession.

Benefits of pets, especially in adversarial 180-degree imposing times

Pets are essential to many people's lives, providing companionship, love, and joy. They offer unconditional love, comfort, and a sense of security and can also positively impact our physical and mental health. They can help to reduce stress, lower blood pressure and decrease feelings of loneliness and isolation. They are not just animals; they are family members and hold a special place in our hearts. The bond between humans and pets is extraordinary and a special relationship by many. Many consider their pets their best friends and would do anything to ensure they are happy and healthy.

As we have seen in previous chapters, the legal education system faces numerous challenges that can significantly impact students' growth and development. From misconceptions and difficulties to limitations of traditional teaching methods, the journey of becoming a legal professional can be a challenging one. But just like our beloved puppy dog, who may wander and hunt for the perfect toy, students too can wander and hunt for the ideal solutions to these challenges. So, just like the puppy dog, who never gives up and always finds the perfect toy, legal students too can find the perfect solutions to the challenges they face in legal education. In the next chapter, we will delve deeper into the specific challenges of time, resources, and spaces that legal students may face. As we follow our puppy dog's journey, we will explore how these challenges can be navigated and how students can be supported in their quest for success in the legal profession.

Chapter Thirteen

Tears in Time, Resources and Spaces

"Divorce is expensive... It's ripping your heart out through your wallet" - Robbin Williams.

In the previous chapters, we have discussed the challenges faced by students in legal education and the impact it can have on their growth and development. This chapter will delve deeper into the specific challenges of time, resources, and spaces that legal students may face. These challenges can include a lack of access to legal help, limited time to complete coursework and internships, and limited physical space for studying and networking.

Once upon a time, in a not-so-distant future, a young boy named Max lived in a coastal town. He loved playing in the sand and swimming in the ocean with his family. They had a beautiful home, a lush yard, and a happy life.

One day, a massive hurricane hit their town, and everything changed. The wind and rain were so strong that Max's home and many others in the neighborhood were completely destroyed. His parents were separated from him during the storm, and he was left alone on the beach, surrounded by debris and destruction.

Max was in shock and didn't know what to do. He wandered the beach, searching for his parents and home, but they were nowhere to be found. He was cold, hungry, and scared. He thought he would never see his parents or his home again.

Just when things seemed hopeless, a rescue team arrived on the beach. They were equipped with advanced technology and could locate Max's parents and bring them back together. They were also able to help Max and his family find a new home, one designed to withstand the powerful storms that were becoming more frequent due to the changing climate.

Max and his family were able to start anew and live in a safe and comfortable home. The new home was built on stilts and had reinforced walls to protect against the wind and the water. It also had a system of solar panels and wind turbines that provided power and water.

Max learned a valuable lesson from experience, the importance of being prepared for natural disasters and sustainable living. He realized that the world was changing and that adapting to the new reality was important. He grew up to be an advocate for sustainable living and disaster preparedness and helped many others in his community to be better prepared for future storms.

Tears in time

Like tearing books in half, one of the biggest challenges faced by legal students is the lack of time to complete coursework and internships. Many students work part-time or full-time jobs while attending law school, which can make it challenging to balance their coursework and internships with their other responsibilities. Additionally, the rigorous nature of legal education can make it difficult for students to find time to study and prepare for exams.

To mitigate this challenge, students can try to prioritize their time and use time management techniques to make the most available time. This can include creating a schedule to plan their time, setting specific daily goals, and using tools such as calendars, to-do lists, and time-tracking apps to stay on track. Additionally, some schools offer support services such as tutoring, mentoring, and counseling to help students manage their time more efficiently.

Once upon a time, a young woman named Sarah had always dreamed of becoming a lawyer. She had worked hard to get into a prestigious law school, but once she got there, she soon realized that the road ahead was going to be challenging.

Like many other legal students, Sarah was faced with the daunting task of balancing her coursework and internships with her other responsibilities. She had a part-time job to pay for her tuition and a family that she needed to take care of. Her days were long and tiring, and she often struggled to keep up with the demands of her classes and her job.

Sarah knew that her legal education was important, but she also knew that she couldn't neglect her other responsibilities. She realized that she needed to find a way to make the most of her limited time. She decided to prioritize her time and use time management techniques to make the most of her available time. She created a schedule to plan her time, set specific daily goals, and used tools such as calendars, to-do lists, and time-tracking apps to stay on track.

Sarah's hard work paid off; she could balance her coursework and internships with her other responsibilities. She did well in her classes and completed her internships on time. Additionally, the school offered support services such as tutoring, mentoring, and counseling which helped her to manage her time more efficiently.

Sarah graduated with honors and landed a job at a top law firm. She looked back on her time in law school and realized that it was not just about the knowledge she acquired but also the skills she had developed, such as time management. She knew that she would need to continue to use these skills throughout.

Tears in resources

Like a bank account ripped in half, another challenge faced by legal students is the lack of access to legal resources. Many students, especially those from low-income backgrounds, may not have the financial resources to purchase the books and materials needed for their coursework and internships. Additionally, many students may not have access to the technology and equipment needed to complete coursework and internships.

To mitigate this challenge, students can seek out resources available at their school, such as financial aid and scholarships, low-cost or free legal resources, and technology loan programs. Additionally, students can network with legal professionals and alums to gain access to resources and opportunities that they may have yet to have access to.

Why did the wallet feel sad?
Because it got torn in half!

Tears in spaces

Limited physical space can be another challenge faced by legal students. Many students may not have access to a dedicated study space or may not have the privacy they need to focus on their coursework and internships. Additionally, students may not have access to spaces where they can network with legal professionals and other students.

To mitigate this challenge, students can seek out resources such as study groups, study rooms, and quiet spaces on campus. Additionally, students can use online resources such as virtual study groups and networking platforms to connect with other students and legal professionals. Some schools also provide counseling and mentoring programs that can help students to manage stress and anxiety caused by limited physical space.

Tears in time, resources, and spaces from family at home

Family responsibilities can also contribute to the challenges of legal students' time, resources, and space. For example, students who are also parents or caregivers may face difficulties balancing their home responsibilities with their school duties. They may have to miss classes or internships to take care of their family or may not have access to the resources and support they need to succeed in their studies.

Additionally, students who come from low-income or single-parent households may also face challenges in terms of time and resources as they may not have the financial or emotional support they need to succeed in their studies. They may have to work multiple jobs to support themselves and their families, which can make it difficult to find time to study and complete coursework.

To mitigate these challenges, students can seek out resources such as childcare, financial aid and scholarships, and counseling services. Additionally, schools and organizations can provide support to students by offering flexible class schedules, online course options, and other resources to help them balance their responsibilities at home with their responsibilities in school.

It's also important to note that legal education providers can change how they teach to consider these different family dynamics in their curriculum. By recognizing the impact of the family at home in legal education, they can create a more inclusive and equitable education system for all students.

Students face many challenges in terms of time, resources, and space. These challenges can have a significant impact on their growth and development. However, by understanding the specific challenges and seeking resources and support, students can mitigate them and navigate their legal education journey. Legal education institutions need to recognize these challenges and provide support to their students in the form of counseling and mentoring—other resources to help them overcome these challenges and succeed in the legal profession.

There's a joke it says, "*So I'm trying to open a chain of outdoor, overnight facilities to help students overcome symptoms of ADHD. Unfortunately, I'm having trouble getting the bank to approve a loan for concentration camps.*

In other words, it is vital for parents, professionals, and organizations all to flex together to provide support and resources to students outside of the traditional legal education system, such as through internship and mentoring programs, experiential learning or shadowing 180- and adaptive 360-degree sides, and networking opportunities. Working together as a revitalization team can create a more inclusive and equitable legal education system for all students.

Chapter Fourteen

How Academic Law Caveats Can Address the Challenges of the Future

"You should never view your challenges as a disadvantage. Instead, it's important for you to understand that your experience facing and overcoming adversity is actually one of your biggest advantages" - Michelle Obama.

In the previous chapters, we have discussed the many challenges faced by legal students, including those related to time, resources, and space. We have also discussed the importance of academic law caveats in revitalizing legal education.

This chapter will explore how theoretical law caveats can address future challenges and create a more inclusive and equitable education system.

In the good old days, education and the professional world would have undergone a significant transformation by now. Gone are the days of one-size-fits-all education and strict professional hierarchies. Instead, a more inclusive and equitable system generally emerges.

In new systems, access is tailored to each student's individual needs and interests. Classes used to be small and interactive, and students were encouraged to work together to solve real-world problems. They were also allowed to pursue internships and apprenticeships aligned with their career goals.

The professional world has evolved to become more inclusive and equitable. Companies and organizations were committed to promoting diversity and equality in the workplace. They offered flexible work arrangements and provided professional development opportunities for employees at all levels.

Why was the businessman's yoga class so profitable?
Because he was always in the "flex-ible" position to make a "stretch" of money!

The legal profession was no exception. The traditional model of legal education was reformed to incorporate more practical and experiential learning opportunities, more focus on alternative dispute resolution methods, and more on understanding legal issues' social and economic context

With this new system in place, people of all backgrounds and abilities had the opportunity to succeed and reach their full potential. This new world was a more just and equitable place where everyone had the chance to succeed, regardless of their background or circumstances.

This story is not meant to be prescriptive. Still, it shows how a more inclusive and equitable education and the professional system can bring benefits to society by providing individuals with the opportunity to reach their full potential and contribute to a more just and fair world.

In this age of legends, a law student named Alice found herself struggling to keep up with her coursework. She was constantly bogged down with case law and statutes and drowning in legal jargon. But one day, she stumbled upon a magical AI assistant named Bob. Bob was a legal coach who could understand her problems and provide her with the resources and support she needed to succeed in her studies.

Bob helped Alice navigate the legal system by breaking down complex legal concepts into simple, easy-to-understand language. He also provided her with access to legal databases and virtual networking platforms, where she could connect with legal professionals and other students.

But Bob wasn't just a legal coach; he was also a master of simulations. He could create virtual legal scenarios that allowed Alice to gain hands-on experience in a safe and controlled environment. Alice was so impressed with Bob's abilities that she decided to take him to class.

When she presented Bob to her classmates, they were all amazed by his capabilities. But their professor was skeptical; he thought that Alice was cheating. But then Bob explained that he was an AI assistant and how he could be used to make legal education more efficient and effective by providing students with access to resources and opportunities that were previously unavailable.

The professor was so impressed by Bob's abilities that he decided to incorporate him into the curriculum. Bob became the most popular professor in the law school, and soon, other law schools began to take notice and followed suit.

Thanks to Bob, Alice graduated at the top of her class and became a successful lawyer. She even went on to create her own legal AI firm and helped other law students navigate the legal system easily. And Bob? He still lives on in the law schools assisting the students to achieve their goals and make legal education more inclusive and equitable.

The importance of interdisciplinary education

One of the key ways in which academic law caveats can address the challenges of the future is through the integration of interdisciplinary education.

This approach recognizes that legal education is about learning the law and understanding the broader social, economic, and political context in which the law operates. By integrating other disciplines, such as psychology, sociology, and political science, students can gain a more holistic understanding of the legal system and be better equipped to address future complex challenges.

In a world where professionals face ever-increasing complexity and change, a young law student named Jackie struggled to keep up. She found herself bogged down in case law and legal theory, needing to understand the broader context in which the law operated. She felt that her legal education needed to be completed and that she needed to be equipped to address the complex legal issues of the future.

One day, Jackie was introduced to the concept of interdisciplinary education and what other professionals were doing independently. She learned that by integrating other disciplines and innovations, such as psychology, sociology, and child safety files, into her legal education, she would gain a more holistic understanding of the legal system and be better equipped to address future complex challenges.

She was excited about the opportunity to learn about the law's social, economic, and political context and how it's related to other fields. She enrolled in classes that provided her with a better understanding of the psychological and social factors that influence legal decision-making and the economic and political forces that shape the legal system

As she progressed through her education, Jackie realized that this interdisciplinary approach gave her a broader and more nuanced understanding of the law. She was able to see the legal system in a new light, and she was better equipped to address the complex legal issues of the future.

Jackie graduated with a well-rounded education and landed a job at a top social justice firm. She applied her interdisciplinary knowledge to her work and became a leading expert in her field. She realized that interdisciplinary education and skills were crucial for addressing future challenges and became an advocate for this approach to legal education.

This story highlights the importance of interdisciplinary education in preparing students to tackle the complexity and ever-changing nature of the legal profession. It also suggests that by looking at the law through different lenses and understanding the broader social, economic, and political context of the law, legal students can become more effective and well-rounded legal professionals.

The role of technology

Another important aspect of academic law caveats is the integration of technology. Technology has the potential to revolutionize the way legal education is delivered and can provide students with access to resources and opportunities that were previously unavailable. For example, through the use of virtual reality, students can experience simulated legal scenarios and gain hands-on experience in a safe and controlled environment. Additionally, online resources such as legal databases and networking platforms can provide students with access to a wealth of information and opportunities to connect with legal professionals and other students.

The importance of diversity and inclusion

Another key way in which academic law caveats can address the challenges of the future is by promoting diversity and inclusion. By creating a more inclusive legal education system, students from diverse backgrounds can have equal access to opportunities and resources. This can be achieved through initiatives such as scholarships, mentoring programs and networking opportunities that are specifically designed to support students from underrepresented groups. Additionally, legal education providers can also ensure that their curriculum is inclusive and reflects the diversity of society.

The role of community engagement

Finally, academic law caveats can address the challenges of the future by promoting community engagement. By connecting legal education with the communities it serves, students can gain a deeper understanding of the real-world challenges faced by individuals and organizations. This can be achieved through initiatives such as pro bono work, community service, and clinical programs. Additionally, law students can also be involved in policy-making and other community-based initiatives that can have a real impact on people's lives.

In conclusion, academic law caveats can play a vital role in addressing the challenges of the future and creating a more inclusive and equitable legal education system. Through the integration of interdisciplinary education, technology, diversity and inclusion, and community engagement, legal education providers can provide students with the skills and resources they need to succeed in the legal profession and make a positive impact on society.

Chapter Fifteen

Examples of Successful Implementation of Family Law Caveats

In the previous chapters, we discussed the many challenges faced by legal students, the importance of academic law caveats in revitalizing legal education, and the various ways they can be implemented to address these challenges. In this chapter, we will explore real-world examples of successful implementation of academic law caveats in legal education and their positive impact on students, legal professionals, and society.

Back in the day, a law school struggled to keep up with the times. Its curriculum needed to be updated, and its students needed hands-on experience to succeed in the legal profession. But one day, the Dean of the law school, Priscilla, had a stroke of genius. She hired a team of tech wizards to give the school a much-needed makeover.

The tech wizards worked their magic. Soon, the law school had a virtual reality program where students could experience mock trials, negotiations, and other legal proceedings in a realistic setting. The students were thrilled; they could finally see how the law worked.

The tech wizards didn't stop there; they also implemented an AI-based legal research system that allowed students to access a vast library of legal resources, including case law and statutes. The students were amazed; they could now research case law and statutes in seconds without the help of a librarian.

But the tech wizards had one more trick up their sleeves; they suggested that the Dean connect the law school with the communities it serves by providing legal assistance to disadvantaged communities through pro bono work and community service. The Dean was hesitant initially, but she gave it a try, and the results were terrific. The students finally saw how the law works in the real world, and the community was grateful for the help.

Thanks to the tech wizards, the law school became the most popular in the country, and soon, other law schools followed in its footsteps. The Dean became a legend in the legal community, and the students became successful AI writers who used the skills she learned to impact society positively

And the tech wizards? Well, they decided to open their own AI tech company and continued to help other law schools to become more efficient and effective. They became known as the "law school teasers."

The use of virtual reality in legal education

One example of successful implementation of academic law caveats is the use of virtual reality in legal education. This technology has been used to create simulated legal scenarios, providing students with hands-on experience in a safe and controlled environment. For example, a law school in the United States has implemented a virtual reality program where students can experience mock trials, negotiations, and other legal proceedings in a realistic setting. This has not only helped students to gain practical experience but also improved their understanding of the legal system and the role of legal professionals in society.

Virtual reality (VR) technology is a valuable tool in helping train new professionals in various fields. One of the critical benefits of VR is that it allows users to experience simulations of real-world situations in a safe and controlled environment. This allows trainees to practice and refine their skills in a way that is impossible with traditional training methods.

In the field of law, virtual reality can be used to simulate courtrooms and other legal settings, allowing law students to practice their courtroom skills and better understand the legal process. This can help students develop the confidence and competence they need to succeed in their careers. Additionally, VR technology can simulate mediation and negotiation scenarios, allowing students to practice these skills in a realistic setting.

Similarly, in engineering, VR can be used to simulate construction sites and other real-world environments. This allows engineering students to practice their skills, such as building design and construction, in a safe and controlled setting. This can help them develop the technical expertise they need to excel in their field.

VR technology is increasingly being used to train pilots to avoid crashes. VR simulators provide a realistic and safe environment for pilots to practice emergency procedures, such as dealing with engine failures or other technical issues and handling difficult weather conditions.

One of the critical advantages of VR training is that it allows pilots to experience a wide range of scenarios in a controlled environment without the risks associated with real-world training. Pilots can practice emergency procedures and decision-making skills in a safe and controlled setting, allowing them to build confidence and competence in handling difficult situations.

Moreover, VR technology allows pilots to experience a level of realism that would be impossible to achieve through traditional training methods, such as using flight simulators or reading manuals. VR headsets provide a fully immersive experience, allowing pilots to look around the virtual cockpit and see all the instruments and controls as they would in a real aircraft. This helps pilots become familiar with the cockpit layout and develop muscle memory for the controls, which can be critical in an emergency situation.

Virtual reality simulates surgeries and other medical procedures in medicine, allowing medical students to practice their skills and gain hands-on experience before working with real patients. This can help them develop a better understanding of the human body and the procedures they will perform, leading to better patient outcomes.

Overall, virtual reality technology is proving to be a valuable tool for training new professionals in various fields. It allows students to practice and refine their skills in a safe and controlled environment, which can help them to develop the confidence and expertise they need to succeed in their careers.

Virtual reality is also helping students who are experiencing homesickness to stay connected with their family and friends. With VR, students can visit their hometowns, neighborhoods, and even their family's homes as if they were there in person. The technology provides an immersive experience that allows students to feel like they are physically present in their hometown, even when they are thousands of miles away.

In addition to visiting their homes, VR allows students to participate in family events, emergency issues, and social activities such as dinner parties, birthdays, holidays, and other special occasions. This can help alleviate feelings of isolation and loneliness and provide students with a sense of connection to their loved ones.

Furthermore, VR can also be used to provide virtual tours of colleges and universities for students who are considering different institutions. This can be particularly beneficial for students who cannot visit campuses in person due to financial or logistical reasons.

Feeling homesick is a common experience for many people, especially those who have left their homes to pursue education or work opportunities. Being away from the familiar comforts of home, family and friends can be difficult and cause sadness, loneliness, and general vulnerabilities.

Pets, like VR preparations, can be an excellent comfort for homesick people. They provide a sense of companionship and familiarity that can help to ease feelings of homesickness. Many people find that pets, such as dogs and cats, can help to fill the void left by the absence of loved ones. They provide comfort and emotional support, which can be particularly helpful during difficult times.

Pets are also great listeners, they never judge, and they are always there to cheer you up. They can make you laugh and also be a source of comfort when you're feeling down. They can also serve as a reminder of home, helping to keep memories of home alive.

In addition to the emotional benefits, pets can also have a positive impact on physical health. Studies have shown that pet ownership can lead to lower blood pressure, reduced stress and anxiety, and improved overall well-being.

Overall, pets can be a valuable asset for those who are feeling homesick. They provide a sense of companionship, comfort, and emotional support that can ease feelings of homesickness and make being away from home easier.

Why did the robot feel homesick?
Because he missed his metal dog.

Overall, VR technology provides new ways to bridge the gap between students, their families, and their friends. It provides a level of connection and immersion that was previously impossible, helping students feel more connected and less homesick while they are away at school.

The use of AI in legal research

Another example of successful implementation of academic law caveats is the use of AI in legal research. This technology has been used to provide students with access to a wealth of legal information and resources, including case law, statutes, and legal databases. For example, a law school in Canada has implemented an AI-based legal research system that allows students to access a vast library of legal resources, including case law and statutes, as well as the ability to connect with legal professionals and other students. This has not only made legal research more efficient but also helped students to develop the critical thinking and analytical skills necessary to succeed in the legal profession.

The use of community engagement

Finally, academic law caveats can be successfully implemented through community engagement. By connecting legal education with the communities it serves, students can gain a deeper understanding of the real-world challenges individuals and organizations face. For example, a law school in Australia has implemented a program where students provide legal assistance to disadvantaged communities through pro bono work and community service. This not only helped students to develop the necessary legal skills but also made a positive impact on the community.

Once upon a time, there were two law students named Bob and Alice. Bob came from a family that had experienced a high-conflict divorce, and as a result, he had a lot of emotional baggage that he carried with him to law school. On the other hand, Alice came from a family with a relatively smooth divorce, and she could focus on her studies without much distraction.

Bob found the traditional legal education system overwhelming and unapproachable, and he often felt lost in class. He struggled to keep up with the readings and assignments and often felt like giving up.

Meanwhile, Alice easily sailed through her classes, and she was always the first to raise her hand with a question or an answer.

One day, the law school introduced a new program focused on integrating scientific laws into family law education. Bob was initially skeptical, but he decided to try it. To his surprise, he found that the program helped him understand his family's situation in a new light and gave him a new perspective on the law. He was able to channel his emotions into his studies, and he soon became one of the top students in his class.

Alice, on the other hand, was not interested in the new program, thinking that she didn't need it, as her family's divorce was already settled and in the past.

She soon found that while she could do well in traditional law classes, she could not understand or connect to her clients in her family law practice as well as her peers who took the new program.

Bob and Alice graduated from law school together but took different paths. Bob became a successful family law attorney known for his empathy and understanding of his client's situations. Alice became a successful traditional lawyer but often struggled to connect with her family law clients.

Bob would often tell her, "You should have joined me in the family law caveat program; it could have helped you to understand the gravity of family law cases and how it impacts families." To which Alice would reply, "I guess I should have listened to you, Bob, but now I know it's never too late to learn."

The use of Welldata

Once upon a time, there was a brilliant engineering student named Aaron. He had always been fascinated by the power of data and technology to change the world. He was determined to find a way to make this power accessible to everyone, not just scientists and academics.

One day, Aaron had an idea for a new kind of technology called "Welldata." He envisioned a system that would allow regular people, like parents, to collect and analyze data about the world around them, just like scientists and academics do. He wanted to give everyone the power to be "quantum layer Taylors" - able to make sense of the vast amounts of data in the world.

Aaron set to work developing Welldata; he had created a system that could collect and analyze data from all kinds of sources - websites, phone apps, and even "unrecognizable data" (UD) that had never been seen before. He made it easy for anyone to use, with simple interfaces and clear explanations.

Soon, Welldata was being used by regular parents, calling themselves "Doctors of data." Academic Ph.D. 's started collecting this data along with the scholarly data on everything from their children's health to the storm safety in their area. They could use the data to make more informed decisions and improve their lives.

Aaron's invention was a huge success. It quickly caught the attention of companies like Amazon, who saw the potential for Welldata to revolutionize how we collect and use data. They offered to buy the technology, but Aaron refused. He wanted to ensure that Welldata remained accessible to everyone, not just big corporations.

So, Aaron started his own company, and Welldata became available to everyone through the internet and beyond. It quickly became one of the world's most popular data-collection and analysis tools, and Aaron became known as a partner in Welldata science.

Thanks to Aaron's vision and hard work, regular people everywhere could now access and use data in ways that were once only possible for scientists and academics. He truly changed the world by making the power of data accessible to all.

Chapter Sixteen

Conclusion

In conclusion, legal education is at a crossroads. The traditional methods of teaching law have become outdated and need to keep up with the rapid changes in society and technology. Students face various challenges, from misconceptions and difficulties to a lack of empathy and communication. These challenges affect their academic performance and their emotional and future well-being.

Similarly, throughout history, other fields of study have undergone similar changes and challenges. For example, in medicine, traditional methods of teaching and practicing medicine were once focused solely on the physical symptoms of illness and disease.

However, as society and technology progressed, it became clear that a more holistic approach was needed. This led to integrating psychology and social sciences into medical education, which helped doctors better understand the emotional and social factors that contribute to a person's overall health and well-being.

Similarly, in education, traditional teaching methods have been challenged by the rapid advancements in technology and the changing needs of students. This has led to a shift towards more interactive and collaborative learning methods and the integration of technology in the classroom.

In all these examples, it is clear that to keep up with the changing times and the needs of society, it is important for fields of study to adapt and evolve. By recognizing and addressing the challenges that arise and by incorporating new knowledge and methods, we can ensure that we provide students with the skills and knowledge they need to succeed in their chosen field and make a positive impact in the world.

Once upon a time, a majestic creature was known as the dinosaur. They roamed the earth for millions of years, dominating the land and sea with their sheer size and strength. But as the earth's climate and environment changed, the dinosaurs failed to evolve and adapt to their new surroundings.

Despite their impressive abilities, they were unable to adapt to the new world around them, and they were slowly pushed to the brink of extinction. Many of the larger dinosaurs, such as the T-Rex and the Brontosaurus, could not find enough food to sustain themselves, and their populations dwindled.

As time passed, the dinosaurs grew fewer and fewer in number until finally; they were no longer to be found on the earth. The once mighty creatures were now nothing more than a distant memory, a cautionary tale of what can happen when a species fails to evolve and adapt to its changing environment.

This story serves as a reminder of the importance of adapting and evolving to survive in a constantly changing world. Just like the dinosaurs, businesses and organizations that fail to evolve and adapt to new technologies, market trends, and societal changes, will eventually become extinct. Those who can learn to adapt and change with the times will thrive.

Academic law caveats offer a solution to these challenges by providing students with the skills and knowledge they need to succeed in the legal profession. By integrating scientific laws into family law education, students can gain a deeper understanding of the law and its impact on society. This can lead to more inclusive and equitable legal education and help students to become more effective and empathetic legal professionals.

Furthermore, academic law caveats also provide a way for legal education to adapt to future challenges. By embracing flexible, conversational AI-like terms and providing more equitable access to legal education, students will be better prepared to meet the demands of the 21st century.

In short, education needs to evolve to keep up with the times, and academic law caveats offer a way forward. By embracing this new approach to legal education, we can help to create a more just and equitable society for all.

Chapter Seventeen

Summary of Key Points

In this book, we have explored the current state of legal education, and the challenges students face. We have also examined the potential of academic law caveats to solve these challenges.

Once upon a time, a group of law students was tired of the traditional methods of teaching law. They felt like they were stuck in a boring and outdated system and longed for something new and exciting.

One day, they stumbled upon a brochure for a new program that focused on integrating scientific laws into family law education. They were intrigued and decided to give it a try.

The program turned out to be a wild ride. They learned about the laws of physics and engineering and how they could be applied to family law cases. They built bridges out of spaghetti and marshmallows to represent mediation agreements and even used LEGOs to construct a skyscraper to represent a child custody case.

The students were having so much fun that they didn't even realize they were learning. They were finally able to understand the law in a way that made sense to them, and they were able to apply it in real-world situations.

Thanks to the new program, they were able to graduate at the top of their class, and they all got great jobs as lawyers. But most importantly, they were able to help their clients more efficiently and effectively.

As they looked back on their law school experience, they all agreed that if it weren't for the program that integrated scientific laws into family law education, they would have never been able to bridge the gap between boring traditional legal education and exciting scientific laws.

The End.

Key points that have been discussed in this book include:

- The traditional methods of teaching law have become outdated, and they are no longer able to keep up with the rapid changes in society and technology.

- Students are facing a wide range of challenges, including misconceptions and difficulties, lack of empathy and communication, and lack of access to legal education.

- Academic law caveats provide a solution to these challenges by integrating scientific laws into family law education and providing students with the skills and knowledge they need to succeed in the legal profession.

- By embracing this new approach to legal education, we can help to create a more just and equitable society for all.

- Academic law caveats also provide a way for legal education to adapt to the challenges of the future by embracing flexible, conversational AI-like terms and providing more equitable access to legal education.

- Successful implementation of academic law caveats in legal education has been shown to have a positive impact on students, legal professionals, and society as a whole.

- It's never too late to learn, and it is possible to bridge the gap between traditional legal education and scientific laws with the help of academic law caveats in order to make a positive impact in society and the legal community.

In summary, the book has highlighted the need for a change in legal education and the potential of academic law caveats as a solution. It shows that with the right approach and mindset, legal education can be revitalized and made more inclusive and effective, helping students become better legal professionals and positively impacting society.

Once upon a time, several children of God were also modern-day civil rights leaders. They were determined to change history and make the world a better place for all people. They suffered greatly for their beliefs and were maladapted for the sake of inequality but never gave up.

One of these leaders was a young woman named Rosa, who refused to give up her seat on a bus to a white person. She was arrested, and her actions sparked a boycott of the buses. Despite her hardships, Rosa continued to speak out against discrimination and fight for civil rights.

Another leader was a man named Martin, who gave powerful speeches and led peaceful protests. He, too, faced many challenges and even violence, but he never wavered in his belief that all people were created equal.

Despite their suffering, Rosa and Martin, along with many other leaders, were able to bring about change. They helped pass laws that ensured equal rights for all, inspiring others to continue the fight for justice.

These leaders, like the Children of Israel in the Bible, were willing to suffer for what they knew was divinely inspired, and through their courage, determination, and faith in God, they were able to change history and make the world a better place for all people.

The story of Rosa and Martin reminds us that even when things seem im possible, we can overcome any obstacle and make a positive change in the world with faith, determination, and courage.

Chapter Eighteen

Future Directions for Revitalizing Education

Together we have highlighted the need for a change in legal education and the potential of academic law caveats as a solution. However, there is still much work to be done in order to fully revitalize legal education. In this chapter, we will explore some of the future directions that can be taken to continue this process.

One key area that needs to be addressed is the integration of technology into legal education. With advances in artificial intelligence, virtual reality, and other technologies, there are many opportunities for legal education to become more interactive and engaging for students. This can also help to bridge the gap between traditional legal education and the rapidly changing technological landscape.

Another area that needs to be addressed is the issue of access to legal education. Many students, particularly those from marginalized communities, face barriers to accessing legal education. This is a problem that needs to be addressed through targeted outreach and support programs.

Additionally, there is a need to continue to integrate scientific laws into family law education and providing students with the skills and knowledge they need to succeed in the legal profession. This can be done through collaborations with other fields such as Industrial/Organizational Psychology,Childhood development, and STEM fields.

Finally, it is important to continue to research and evaluate the impact of academic law caveats on legal education. This will help to identify areas for improvement and to ensure that the changes being made are having the desired effect.

In conclusion, revitalizing legal education is a complex and ongoing process. However, by embracing new technologies, increasing access to legal education, and continuing to integrate scientific laws into family law education, we can create a more inclusive and effective legal education system that prepares students to meet the challenges of the future.

Once upon a time, in a land known as America, there was a line of heroes who stood up for inclusivity against all odds. These heroes came from all walks of life, but they all shared a common goal: to create a society where everyone had an equal opportunity to succeed.

At the head of this line of heroes was a young lawyer named Samantha. She had grown up in a marginalized community and had witnessed firsthand the barriers that many people faced when trying to access legal education. Determined to make a change, she decided to attend law school and become an advocate for inclusivity in the legal profession.

While in law school, Samantha faced many challenges. She was often the only person of color in her class and was frequently met with resistance from her professors and classmates. But she refused to be discouraged. Instead, she used her experiences to fuel her passion for creating a more inclusive legal education system.

After graduating from law school, Samantha went on to become a successful lawyer and an advocate for inclusivity. She worked tirelessly to increase access to legal education for marginalized communities and to create a more equitable legal profession.

Samantha was not alone in her fight. Alongside her stood a diverse group of heroes, each with their own unique stories and struggles. There was a social worker named Maria, who fought to improve the lives of immigrants and refugees. There was a teacher named Jake, who worked to create more inclusive and equitable classrooms. And there was a community organizer named Ahmed, who worked to empower marginalized communities and give them a voice in the political process.

Together, these heroes stood up against discrimination and prejudice, and they refused to back down. They fought for what they believed in, and their efforts began to pay off. Slowly but surely, they were able to create a more inclusive and equitable society.

Thanks to their efforts, many people who had been previously excluded from the legal profession were now able to access legal education and become lawyers. Communities that had been ignored and marginalized were now being heard and their rights were being protected.

The line of heroes never gave up and their legacy continues to inspire new generations to fight for inclusivity, equity and to build a better future for all.

Chapter Nineteen

Call to Action for Students, Parents and Institutions

Together we have been to the mountain and can go down the other side. We highlighted the need for a change in legal education and the potential of academic law caveats as a solution. However, much work still needs to be done to fully revitalize legal education. In this chapter, we will explore some of the future directions that can be taken to continue this process.

One key area that needs to be addressed is technology integration into legal education. With advances in artificial intelligence, virtual reality, and other technologies, legal education has many opportunities to become more interactive and engaging for students. This can also help to bridge the gap between traditional legal education and the rapidly changing technological landscape.

Another area that needs to be redressed is the issue of access to legal education. Many students, particularly those from marginalized communities, face barriers to accessing legal education. This is a problem with known solutions that need to be addressed through targeted outreach and support programs.

Additionally, there is a need to continue integrating scientific laws into family law education and provide students with the skills and knowledge they need to succeed in the legal profession. This can be done through collaborations with other fields, such as Industrial/Organizational Psychology, Childhood development, and STEM.

Finally, it is important to continue researching and evaluating the impact of academic law caveats on legal education. This will help identify areas for improvement and ensure that the changes being made have the desired effect.

In conclusion, revitalizing education is a complex and ongoing process. However, by embracing new technologies, increasing access to legal education, and continuing to integrate scientific laws into family law education, we can create a more inclusive and effective legal education system that prepares students to meet future challenges.

Long ago, in a land known as America, there was a line of heroes who stood up for inclusivity against all odds. These heroes came from all walks of life, but they all shared a common goal: to create a society where everyone had an equal opportunity to succeed.

At the head of this line of heroes was a young lawyer named Samantha. She had grown up in a marginalized community and witnessed firsthand the barriers many people faced when accessing legal education.

Determined to make a change, she decided to attend engineering and law school and became a new school advocate for inclusivity in the legal profession.

While in school, Samantha faced many challenges. She was often the only person of color in her class and was frequently met with resistance from her professors and classmates. But she refused to be discouraged.

Instead, she used her experiences to fuel her passion for creating a more inclusive legal education system.

After graduating, Samantha became a successful Family Law 2.0 lawyer and an advocate for superior inclusivity. She worked tirelessly to increase access to legal education for marginalized communities and to create a more equitable legal profession.

Samantha was not alone in her fight. Alongside her stood a diverse group of heroes, each with unique stories and struggles. There was a social worker named Maria who fought to improve the lives of immigrants and refugees. There was a teacher named Jake who worked to create more inclusive and equitable classrooms. And there was a community organizer named Ahmed who worked to empower marginalized communities and give them a voice in the political process.

Together, these heroes stood up against discrimination and prejudice and refused to back down. They fought for what they believed in, and their efforts began to pay off. Slowly but surely, they were able to create a more inclusive and equitable society.

Thanks to their efforts, many people who had been previously excluded from the legal profession could now access legal education and become lawyers. Communities that had been ignored and marginalized were now being heard, and their rights were being protected.

The line of heroes never gave up, and their legacy inspires new generations to fight for inclusivity and equity and build a better future for all.

Chapter Twenty

References

1966 debate over the First Law School in America: William & Mary law school. Site. (n.d.). Retrieved January 12, 2023, from https://scholarship.law.wm.edu /lawschooldebate1966/

Boon, G., needer, H., Midnight, Sam, J., Bob, Me, Kadence, guy, T. bridge, Olive, wolf, M. the, Lola, Frenchy, Garret, & Marques, B. (2021, December 3). Garrett Boon. Garrett's Bridges: Resources to Help You Build a Model Bridge. Retrieved January 11, 2023, from https://www.garrettsbridges.com/design/t heforces/

Cover image courtesy: Photo by RODNAE Productions: https://www.pe xels.com/photo/man-woman-school-gift-7713345/

Definitions of fact, theory, and law in scientific work: National Center for Science Education. Definitions of Fact, Theory, and Law in Scientific Work | National Center for Science Education. (n.d.). Retrieved January 12, 2023, f r o m https://ncse.ngo/definitions-fact-theory-and-law-scientific-work#:~:text=Law %3A%20A%20descriptive%20generalization%20about,%2C%20inferences%2 C%20and%20tested%20hypotheses.

DOE explains...Quantum computing. Energy.gov. (n.d.). Retrieved January 11, 2023, from https://www.energy.gov/science/doe-explainsquantum-computing

Former Whittier Law School. Whittier College. (n.d.). Retrieved January 11, 2023, from https://www.whittier.edu/about/lawschool#:~:text=Kennedy%20formally%20dedicated%20the%20campus,all%20operations%20in%20July%202020.

Newton's first law of Motion. The Physics Classroom. (n.d.). Retrieved January 11, 2023, from https://www.physicsclassroom.com/class/newtlaws/Lesson-1/Newton-s-First-Law

Newton's laws define our architectural design - 4 laws define our architectural design on the at. Studocu. (n.d.). Retrieved January 11, 2023, from https://www.studocu.com/en-us/document/california-state-polytechnic-university-pomona/structures-1/4-newtons-laws-define-our-architectural-design/2956068

About Author

Safeguard your dreams!

Being Least Commanded (Matthew 5:19) has always been an unfair advantage for my colleagues and me, and an "unfair" advantage for systems that hold fast to making labels above us all. We love uncovering the hidden data which is always glossed over a little or glossed over a lot with other adversarial places.

- Hi, I'm Aaron Wemple. Least Commanded author and the founder of Life Winks LLC. I never asked for this, and would rather pray for my shortcomings than talk about myself, but now I love transforming dreams, victim-proofing files & filling in missing organic data ramps, talents, and laws for those with special needs. I also project manage private data metrics for the united CLU parents group and the Future of Data Challenge ReboundHero project. I am best known for following Jesus despite all others, inventing constructive Child Safety Files, which were designed for industrial strength to help divorced or separated parents keep their children ultra-safe during high-conflict adversarial compulsions, and for co-parenting two very intelligent and very talented kids. I am passionate about helping families in need and nonprofits that strive to make a difference in the lives of those who are struggling. I believe that every family deserves to be happy and ultra-safe, and I will continue to work hard to make this a reality for as many disadvantaged heroes as possible.

- I'm partially disabled now, but I previously worked as Facility Administrator at Old Kings Orchard Community Center, TV Director at Maranatha Church, Electrical Designer with CSI, and sheet metal tradesman with Local 36. My academic study includes a bachelor spanning engineering and psychology from SIU-E, Organizational Leadership at Millikin University, and Electrical Engineering at SIU-E. I work with Paraquad in St Louis, The Family Cafe in Florida, and other ability groups to try and regain some sense of independence.

In recent years, my partners in data and I've been recognized by several news leaders, book reviewers, and government organizations for childhood, family, and community-building efforts – 2020 KPLR-TV/YouTube "Morning Blend" interview with Producer James Thomas; 2019 WAND-TV News "Spring Into Action;" 2018 WAND-TV News "Cleaning Up the Book of Justice;" 2017 WAND-TV News "Clean Child Support Initiative; " 2020 Amazon book and university-lead project "Law & Side-Law."

So now I love ensuring good family performance data stays together organically and partnering with license and data development specialists who are interested in the purpose of "twinning greatness" for special needs people socially. We do this to prevent trauma through our proprietary #NewDeals #PracticingSmall and #SavingLives.

Yes, there are floods and curbs, and life can be a pain, but safeguard your dreams and journey with Talentism anyway. Because everything twins greatness!

Also By

Change the Game: One Simple New Deal With Welldata Can Help Anyone Change Break Free Series:

Breaking the Mold: Transforming Legal Learning with Professional Law Caveats - Family Law 2.0 Second Edition

Faithfinder: Inclusive Holiday Stories Empower Readers to Find Their Super-faith!

Impossible Data: How Making Almighty Data Cavityism History Can Help Us Live A Better Life

Impossible Psychologies – Award Yourself Making Mental Cavityism History

Impossible Sociologies

Parenting 2.0 For Un-Haters

Pivoting Impossible Brothers: Award Yourself Kids Making Sibling Cavityism History

Revitalizing Education: The Role of Academic Law Caveats in Student Growth

Outside The Series:

American Pros

Family Law 2.0

I R "Freestyle" Physics – The Study of of Transformation and/or Transfiguration

Law & Side-Law

The Law Doctor

Upbright USA

REVITALIZING EDUCATION

United CLU Parents Guide

Made in the USA
Monee, IL
04 November 2026

67386437R00075